WHAT HAVE WE LEARNED SO FAR?

*Collaborative thoughts on why we are here,
what we're supposed to do while we're here,
and other questions*

Organized by Paul Jackson and
written by the amazing WHWLSF team

ISBN: 978-0-578-42154-4

Interior Design by Booknook.biz.

CONTENTS

INTRODUCTION

In the summer of 2017, I found myself spending time thinking about what I was "supposed" to be doing. I've always felt that we are here for a reason and that the measure of a life is how well we live our lives toward that purpose.

In the past several years and over most of my lifetime, I've spent a fair amount of effort trying to figure things out, but, in the summer of 2017, I was feeling a bit discouraged, run down, and oftentimes caught up in the hopelessness and pessimism of many of my friends about the events of the day and what those events meant about the human condition.

I can't really remember how I came up with the idea of a collaborative writing project to see if a group of people working through the same questions might provide each other with insights, but there are four books that influenced me to initiate this project.

The first and greatest is Victor Frankl's *Man's Search for Meaning*. Frankl believed that we as humans have an innate need for purpose – as important to us as food, protection from the elements, and procreation. Frankl believed that people's meaning was individual to them. They need to figure it out themselves and then live their lives according that meaning. Since I felt a bit stuck, I thought, why not come up with a way to find out what others have figured out?

The second was Jim Holt's book *Why Does the World Exist?: An Existential Detective Story*. In this book, Jim Holt interviews some of the smartest people in the world about the big questions about how we got here, why we are here, and what else is out there. This is a great book and I recommend it, but, as a spoiler alert – no one knew the answers. In fact, all these scientists, philosophers, and learned people emphasized that the more they learned, the less they knew – about the answers and even the questions. So, if the scientists and philosophers haven't figured it out but had fun trying, how about trying a different approach?

The third was Jennifer Rubin's *The Happiness Project* in which the author spent a year trying different happiness techniques – one each month. As part of the project, she created a blog and created a discussion on each of the twelve techniques and incorporated some of the contributors' comments in her book. Keith Richards similarly made effective use of other people's recollections in his autobiography, *Life*. This gave me the idea that maybe there's more (or a different) wisdom in a collaborative thinking and writing exercise.

So, on August 6, 2017, I put my thoughts together and started a project titled: "*What have you learned so far*" (subsequently retitled "*What have we learned so far?*"). Over the next 12 months, I posed a series of questions to my collaborators who provided their thoughts over eight rounds of questions. For the first round I waited with trepidation to see if anyone would participate – but they did! And did they ever! My inarticulate first communication trying to explain an idea I hadn't even thought through resulted in responses and ideas that gave me so much joy and reassurance to know that the questions I had where very similar to the questions other people had.

In most ways, I think our lives are mostly solitary experiences. We yearn for connection, but our brains are evolutionarily guided toward ego-centered self-preservation. At the same time, we also have the capacity to form families, clans, and societies based on mutual interest. One of our greatest capacities is to be able to write things down so other people in different place and times can read them. Mostly this is a solitary experience on the writer's part. Maybe there's an opportunity, through collaborative writing, to come to a better level of understanding of ourselves as we relate to others.

All profits from sales of this book go to the not-for-profit: *For Love of Children* (www.FLOC.org).

So here is our first humble effort. I hope you like it!

What Have We Learned So Far?

ROUND 1: *IS THERE A POINT?*

We started our project in August 2017. I asked for questions from participants with the notion that we can find meaning by asking good questions. Based on responses, I provided the following initial prompts:

"We make our world significant by the courage of our questions and by the depth of our answers" (Carl Sagan)

"Ask and it will be given to you; seek and you will find; knock and the door will be opened to you." (Matthew 7:7)

And the following questions:

Question 1: Is there a purpose to our lives? What makes you think one way or another? Do you recall the point in your life that you came to this view? What shaped your view?

Question 2: In recent years, many (most?) of us in this country and, in a larger sense, the world, have come to live in one "bubble" or another. Whether this bubble is based on political views, religion, geography, socio-economics, or some other factor or factors, we often only hear from people who share our world view, leading to greater and greater divisions among us. What can we do to burst these bubbles and gain a greater understanding of each other?

Question 3: For the believers: What does "*the kingdom is at hand*" mean? To me this implies a sense of urgency and immediacy that I do not perceive in myself or others. What if the Kingdom is already here and what does this imply?"

Question 4: What do you think the key to the universe is that Bruce Springsteen found "in the engine of an old parked car" (from "Growin' Up" from the album Greetings from Asbury Park).

And here are the responses, separated by "‿"

‿

Responses to Question 1:

Why are we here? Is there a purpose? This is something that I think about almost daily, but for me I end up asking "**What are we?**". We can look at life on Earth and see incredible diversity of plants and animals, and we know that we too are animals. We are mammals and called human. Humans are different from other animals. With our continuing array of ideas, technology, and things we are capable of manipulating the physical world in amazing ways. However, I believe that humanity›s great hubris is to think that we are «more intelligent» of better than the animals. I believe animals have emotions and souls. We see now extinction, and the decimation of habitats, the pollution. What right do we have to hurt our fellow lifeforms for our perceived benefit? Of course, this is coming from someone who enjoys a good green chile cheeseburger. So I will touch on the "kingdom of heaven" here. In the book of

Genesis, it is written that God told us the world is ours and all the plants and animals in it. It has always been clear to me that we were expected to be good stewards, and not that this gives us a blank check to do whatever we want. I see the kingdom of heaven as the beautiful bountiful world we were gifted to exist in. We have not been good stewards, and we see now the unprecedented dangers that result. I think it is fine to manipulate the world, including animals, but only if it is done in a responsible way.

But what the heck are we?!! This boggles me when I try to think of it. We know we are carbon-based bipeds, just another of the many species of animals. However, we are so different than the other creatures. I saw some amazing photos from the Cassini probe to Saturn. My favorite was the little dot called Earth as seen from the orbit of Saturn. With our "knowledge" based on our observation going back thousands of years we see we are in a very very big "place". The solar system, the galaxy, and look, there are so many galaxies, and the universe. . .and where does it end? An age old paradoxical question. The notion of us having comprehension of infinity is, well, problematic. I think of the quote "ashes to ashes, dust to dust" and simultaneously the knowledge that life started here from dust in the stars. We are literally stardust. As these ideas bounce around in my mind, I realize that I am "conscious" that I am an organism. This further blows my mind. It's as though it is almost too much to be aware of the things we are. I can become almost paralyzed existentially by these thoughts. One could conclude that there is no purpose, and we just happened, and it's all random. Yet I can't say that without more information, and that information may be unknowable to us. I think most people have an innate sense of immediate purpose, right and wrong, good and bad, etc. Our built in need to survive and procreate, like all plants and animals. I think while we move through the world engaged with day to day life, we are focused on the immediate, and deep questions take a back burner. However, I sometimes feel kind of insane because every day I think of "what are we? What is this?". It is somehow scary to think you are just a temporary being, so small and vulnerable, and without certainty about what we are and why we are here. At my supply shop, I saw a little sign that says "You're a meat coated skeleton made from stardust, riding a rock, hurtling through space. Fear nothing." For me these thoughts are powerful, and freaky. At times I wish I could be less aware of all these thoughts, and more like an animal going about its affairs.

I do not know why we are here, but suspect it is not random, and that we (if we are lucky) find our purpose and fulfill it. I do not know what we are, but when engaged in my purpose I am not plagued by these mysterious questions. I believe we are born who we are. Less so that our environment shaped us. Of course it does, but I see myself drawn to the same things I was drawn to as a young child. I used to pretend I was an archeologist, digging in construction sites. I also really liked the grounds at Leisure World as a child. Now I am a landscaper and work in gardens and forests with plants and soil. I collected rocks, and shiny metal things. Eventually I carved stone and later started making jewelry. As a child my favorite "toys" were the toolbox and coffee percolator. After college I became a barista, and now have a building full of tools and a workshop full of specialized equipment. These are just some examples from my life, and the longer I live the more I see that living is the process of becoming yourself. You are born who you are and hopefully become a fuller and fuller version of yourself by following your purpose. Not everyone feels like they have a purpose, or that there is any in life. Others are not in touch with themselves, and find purposes that don't fulfill them, or even purposes that harm them or others.

Whatever life is, I'll take it. We know no other existence, though it may exist. I choose to not take it all too seriously, and do my best becoming myself. Even though there is unspeakable suffering and unthinkable actions, there is also immense beauty and pleasure. People are capable of being angels and of being demons.

Our technology is incredible, but our collective purpose is scrambled. We have not made the world a better place. We can do and build incredible things, yet continue to kill each other, hurt our environment, have poverty and greed, etc. To me a lot of this computer and "smartphone" business is a stupid and needless filter through which people are living the same lives as before. What makes it better? Is faster better? Is being disengaged from your world and surroundings better? Are you more connected than ever with people in some way, while the big irony stands like an elephant in the room - that connectivity is made through the digital filter and through disconnection with one's world. To the "bubble" question we certainly have plenty of examples of what NOT to do if you want to pop the bubbles and reach a better understanding of one another, and to get back to our collective purpose which I propose as this: To maintain and take care of our world which has all the potential of becoming the kingdom of heaven. It's all up to us! Look what we were given, and what we have done with it. While looking at all the problems facing the world it is easy to get overwhelmed. Remember the best and perhaps only way to change the world is by changing yourself. As a bumper sticker I see says "*Be the change you want to see in the world*".

⁓

Having lived the formative years of my life jumping between different faith systems, growing disillusioned and drifting toward agnosticism then atheism, actively opposing all forms of organized religion only to find faith in my late 30s, I believe in a higher purpose for our existence. We are given the gift of live, not solely to pursue our worldly needs and wants, but to recognize our Creator and to live in such a way that, on one hand, enables us to better withstand the challenges of life and, on the other, prepares and qualifies us for a future existence. Much like the larvae stage of Monarch butterfly's life is a transitional period in its existence, this brief worldly life is also a transitional period in human existence.

~

I believe there is a purpose to our lives. Certainly, this was implanted in me early by nuns but I have also come to see this is true through life itself and voluminous reading of other people's biographies. I recall that I was quite young when I came to this view-certainly 1st grade. This point and it involves interacting lovingly with our fellow human beings/animals on this planet. The purpose in life is relationships. That's why when I become aware of a dying person with absolutely no relationships I feel sad.

~

As a believer in God (the One of many names) and as a believer in evolution, It seems to me that all of creation is and comes from a divine source and is constantly "becoming", moving toward greater consciousness and transcendence. One necessary corollary of this is that we/everyone/everything come from the same Source. In a very deep way, we are all one and dependent upon one another. If this true, then my well-being depends on the well-being of all others. The more others thrive, then the more I thrive. Just the opposite of zero sum suppositions. It follows then that nonviolent living is essential. To destroy/hate/resent others would be a form of hating myself. How can I live conscientiously? How can I live in a way that furthers the evolution of love? How can I live mindful of the value of all creation? These are the questions I struggle with. In a way, I don't need to "do" anything. I don't make things evolve. That process created me, not the other way around. So I more need not to impede, not to get in the way, not to push the river. Yet I, as do we all, have a necessary part to play...to act with love and hope and faith and gratitude. To seek justice for all. To resist the powerful forces of racism (all "isms") and fear and violence.

How do I know that these beliefs are true? Is there even a possibility of proof? So many brilliant thinkers have grappled with these issues and most, I think, have ended up believing in both love and goodness. That the good life is the loving life.

I'd like to offer two quotations.

"Being arches itself
over the vast abyss.
Ah the ball that we dared,
that we hurled into infinite space,
doesn't it fill our hands
differently with its return:
heavier by the weight
of where it has been." (Rilke)

~

"To live in this world
you must be able
to do three things:
to love what is mortal;
to hold it
against your bones knowing
your own life depends on it;

and when the time comes to let it go,
to let it go." (Mary Oliver)

~

Many years ago, I faced a difficult personal crisis. To help work my way through this I saw a very good—but rather unconventional—psychotherapist. Among the many technique she employed was something called 'rebirthing.' The technique involves taking rapid, linked breaths to induce hyperventilation and ultimately an altered state of consciousness. The second time I did this I had the only mystical experience I have ever had. As I lay there conscious but unconscious and unable to move, I became aware of a brightness and 'heard' this question: what if this is how it is *supposed* to be? There was no brightness and no one else heard anything. But I 'saw' and 'heard.'

The question is profound to me for several reasons. If something is 'supposed to be,' then someone, some mind, something must 'intend.' Who or what is this? Whatever it is, it must be intimately involved with me. I have never felt that the intention was for anything other than my good. If this intended good is true for me, then I believe it is true for everyone. How are our lives related that this can be so?

The question also forces me to consider how something can be painful, immoral, evil, bad and yet 'supposed to be'. And more, 'supposed to be' for my good. My resolution is that actions and experiences have to be evaluated not in themselves—or at least not solely—but in relation to the changes they bring about. A boulder in the stream 'bruises' the water but may divert it to a better, more useful path.

In my own case, the crisis I faced and the changes resulting from it greatly changed my life for the better. Those changes would never have happened without such a confrontation. I try to remember this all the time.

As I think about this experience, I am reminded of the Biblical story of Joseph whom his brothers sold into Egyptian slavery. Years later when famine struck, the brothers came to Egypt to buy grain to avoid starvation. Joseph knows them, but they don't recognize him. Eventually he reveals himself to them with the words, you meant it for evil against me, but God meant it for good.

And from the New Testament, *"And we know that in all things God works for the good of those who love him, who have been called according to his purpose."*

～

I think I've always felt that there's a purpose. Much of the time, however, I struggle to know what that meaning and purpose is – that's why I'm excited about this project. When I think about whether there is meaning and purpose, I think about music – to me there's no way there can't be meaning to my life when I can experience the music of Bach (Suite #3 in D Major), Jimi Hendrix (Little Wing), Alison Krauss (Every Time You Say Goodbye) and so much incredible music. I have felt transported to another reality a few times when experiencing an incredible song – either live or recorded. To me, nothing so beautiful and transcendental could come from purposelessness. I hope that participants of this project will share those things that can take them into "another world."

～

Responses to Question 2:

In recent years, many (most?) of us in this country and, in a larger sense, the world, have come to live in one "bubble" or another. Whether this bubble is based on political views, religion, geography, socio-economics, or some other factor or factors, we often only hear from people who share our world view, leading to greater and greater divisions among us. What can we do to burst these bubbles and gain a greater understanding of each other?

~

So, I have an idea here – how about someone – maybe Facebook or Google comes up with a website or app that allows people to have a one on one conversation with someone outside their comfort zone? Nationalists talk to immigrants, top 1%'ers talk to people in poverty, etc. etc. The sponsor could help with ground rules, sample questions, interventions, anonymizing conversations, etc.

~

Get outside of the bubble! Work and do activities outside of your friend/family group. I certainly have patiently listened while patients tell me how much they like/respect some issue/person I disagree with. Ethically I cannot respond so I listen. And I get it. I don't see it their way, but I get it. Occasionally I even change my mind. For example, after seeing several medical-ethical dilemmas regarding abortion, I changed my mind and am in favor of legal abortion. And abortion is an issue on which I think very few people change their mind.

~

How do we burst the "bubbles" we live in, and make a greater effort to bridge the divide we experience and thereby achieve better relationships with people we know and cultivate understanding of those we do not? The goal of this, simply put, is peace and harmony. That is, peace and harmony both inside oneself and with others. There is a rather old song "Walk a

Mile in My Shoes" by Joe South (1969). The lyrics mirror the difficult days of discourse or lack thereof during the Vietnam War. And if people viewed The Vietnam War documentary just aired on PBS, they would have an inkling of how complicated the upheaval was in our country back then. Anyway, the lyrics, in part, are:

"If I could be you, if you could be me for just one hour
If we could find a way to get inside each other's mind, mmmm
If you could see you through my eyes instead of your ego
I believe you'd be surprised to see that you've been blind, mmmm

Walk a mile in my shoes, walk a mile in my shoes
Hey, before you abuse, criticize and accuse
Walk a mile in my shoes."

I find these lyrics apropos to so much that has broken down in our country or seems to be broken down. The divide is not all that wide across millions of people and thousands of miles. When individuals and groups do enter into genuine conversations (not finger-pointing stuff that masquerades as "talking" with people), they seem to see that they have more in common that issues of disagreement. The very words we choose can be inflammatory, without our even realizing it. (Aside: Years ago, I was firmly criticized for referring to myself as being "colorblind" – a term my African American close friend used to describe me! I never have used that term again in a similar context, and I am more than okay with that.)

How to gain better relationships/ build better bridges? First, I think is having a desire to do so is a great start. Then, becoming a well-rounded reader or listener. If things ae to improve, then it is important to read, read a lot. Books, magazine articles, newspapers, thoughtful blogs on a multitude of topics—

all inform us as individuals and as society. Reading requires us to slow down and think – a good thing, yes? But it is important to read items one might not ordinarily read and to assign ourselves some new topics. In the past year, I assigned myself a reading list: The Dying Grass, a novel by William Vollman that goes deeply into the Nez Perce Wars. Also, I have just finished rereading The Known World by Edward P. Jones, taking place in antebellum Virginia, wherein blacks are themselves slaveholders. Anything by Ta-Nahesi Coates is worth the reading and discussion.

~

The very quick answer to how we burst out of these bubbles is to expose yourself to experiences that don't validate your bubble. One way I have successfully been able to break out of my bubble is through charity work. I've been to Haiti for mission trips several times. The realities of day to day living in Haiti is so profoundly different that it doesn't take long to lose touch of your normal day-to-day reality – your bubble.

If you are familiar with Maslow's hierarchy of needs. Life in Haiti is very much centered on the bottom level – physiological needs. Life is very hard there and people spend their days trying to secure very basic needs. It is a very stark contrast to life here where we are on the higher rungs of Maslow's hierarchy – esteem and self-actualization. By spending time sharing meals, working side by side, playing with the Haitians, you end up realizing that though our worlds are very different, at the end of the day there is so much that is the same. All people want to have a way to earn the money they need to provide for themselves and their families. All people want to be treated with dignity and kindness. All people want their kids to be safe and learn and to find a better future. All kids like to play soccer and with water balloons and coloring books.

In a way, the way to burst your bubble is to find the things that make you and the people/things outside of your bubble the same. Then those outside of your bubble are inside of it, and the walls of the bubble break down.

Some quotes that I like that speak to this:

Barack Obama –

"...none of these challenges can be met unless we see ourselves as part of something bigger than our own experience...Our values call upon us to care about the lives of people we will never meet."

Ellen DeGeneres –

"And I believe we can all come together because if you take away the labels, you realize we're far more alike than we are different."

I love Maya Angelou's poem Human Family- (first and last stanzas included)

I note the obvious differences
in the human family.
Some of us are serious,
some thrive on comedy.

Some declare their lives are lived
as true profundity,
and others claim they really live
the real reality.

The variety of our skin tones
can confuse, bemuse, delight,

brown and pink and beige and purple,
tan and blue and white.

I note the obvious differences
between each sort and type,
but we are more alike, my friends,
than we are unalike.

We are more alike, my friends,
than we are unalike.

We are more alike, my friends,
than we are unalike.

~

Responses to Question 3: For the believers: What does "*the kingdom is at hand*" mean?

~

Although I am not a "Endtimes" person, I had always thought of it as something that was not yet here? But could come at any point. So be ready i.e. living a good life. Having said that, I don't believe in the existence of Hell

~

This question resonates with me. I have three frames of references for this question – the Iris Dement song, "The Kingdom has already come" with the lyrics "*but life is waiting just behind that veil. The soul is left to struggle segregated. Trapped in the harbor too weighted.*" I think she's saying that we don't see things the way they are. In Ian McEwen's book "In Paradise", the main character describes an alternate interpretation of the story of Jesus and the "Good Thief":

"Christ crucified is importuned by a penitent thief, in agony on his own cross on that barren hillside. "I beseech you, Jesus, take me with you this day to Paradise!" In traditional gospels, Jesus responds, "Though shalt be with me this day in Paradise," but in older texts – Eastern Orthodox or the Apocrypha, perhaps? – Christ shakes his head, saying, "No friend, we are in Paradise right now."

Lastly, I think about Milton's quote: *"The mind is its own place and in itself, can make a Heaven or Hell, a Hell of Heaven."* Maybe the point here is that we should live to create God's kingdom on earth and should have an immediacy to it – it's not in another place and in an afterlife – its right here – and our responsibility to realize that. I just don't know how.

~

Responses to Question 4: What do you think the key to the universe is that Bruce Springsteen found *"in the engine of an old parked car"*

~

I struggled with this one because I really don't know what Bruce meant, so I'll have to try to project Bruce. I think the protagonist initially rebels from everything but to some degree comes around and recognizes that truth/meaning is out there but overlooked. He recognizes that the answer (the engine) is already built but not in use. He discovers the truth in something that has been silenced (an old parked car). What is that truth? I don't know - the engine is already there but is not being used – the solution is there but has been forgotten or temporarily disregarded (parked). That's all I got. I'm interested in what other people think. Either way – great song.

~

I think Bruce found/had the FREEDOM to live his life the way he wanted instead of the way other people wanted. To go where he wanted, do what he wanted. Because what he found in the in the engine was a key. A key to a old parked car gives you the freedom to go anywhere you want whenever you want. So that you can pull up when they say pull down, you can stand up when they say stand down and you can throw up when they say come down.

ROUND 2: *SO, WHAT ARE WE SUPPOSED TO DO?*

Round 1 focused on "*Is there purpose to our lives?*" so, for round two, we tried to find out how to find our purpose. Additionally, we discussed the notion of "bubbles" that separate us. In late October 2017, I posed the following questions to the team:

> **Question 1:** If you answered "yes" or "maybe" - How do you find out what your purpose is (or if you have a purpose)? If you have "figured it out" – please hold off for the time being, we'll get to that next month.
>
> If you answered "no" – how do you approach your life (i.e. what are you supposed to do in a non-purposeful life?)"
>
> **Question 2:** Last month's second question was: "What can we do to burst these bubbles and gain a greater understanding of each other" Building off this question, what do you think we would find if we were able to completely know one another?
>
> **Question 3:** Do you think there such a thing as a unique, individual "soul"?
>
> **Question 4:** In the Gnostic gospel of Thomas, Jesus said, "Let him who seeks continue seeking until he finds. When he finds, he will become troubled. When he becomes

troubled, he will be astonished, and he will rule over the All." What do you think the seeker finds?

~

Responses to Question 1:
All my working life I felt like I had a job that gave my life a big chunk of its purpose. Helping people, being part of the search for the cure for cancer/HIV/blood disorders, being part of a team I loved etc. Then I changed jobs and all of sudden felt like my work-life had no purpose. In hindsight, (now that you pointed it out!) I think that was a big part of why I hated that job so much. I could have put up with the other negative factors if I felt like it had a purpose other than just a paycheck. Now (Thank God) I am back in a job where I feel like I am "helping" people and my entire life seems to have more purpose.

I also think when your kids are little, you could automatically feel like your life has purpose because they need you for everything. When they grow up, you could feel like your life has less purpose because they are doing just fine without you. Which is good; that was your goal all along. Now they need to find <u>their</u> purpose. But you need to find something to supplement your sense of purpose.

I answered yes, but…my son was in an irreverent play "Avenue Q." One of the puppet's, Princeton, sings a song "Gotta Find My Purpose." Princeton has no idea what to do with his life? He interacts with the other puppets-a conservative, a goof-off, a kindergarten teacher, a "slut" etc. and eventually determines that in the real world, sometimes you never find your purpose. That living life well can be a purpose in and of itself.

~

I would have answered "no" based on my belief that there is no higher authority ruling my life on Earth. That said, I do believe that one should seek a purpose for their life on Earth as a responsibility for sharing a planet with other beings. We are all responsible for each other and to make the planet last for generations to come. As we as a people degenerate into a mind set of "me first" we risk the planet's life, which then shortens the future of human life. We lose our humanity by focusing on our own needs and wants.

I live my life by being aware of others and trying to help where and when I can. I could, of course, do so much more, but life, too, is also about enjoying each day and seeing the beauty of nature and exploring the world to reinforce that people are basically the same in any culture, with the leaders being the people that have generally lost focus on the purpose of their position – to guide and nurture their people and limited resources for the betterment of all, not just to increase their own power and wealth.

Your question is phrased to assume that if one does not believe there is a purpose to one's life then they will pursue a non-purposeful life. I believe you can define your own purpose in life without it being pre-ordained or designated from a higher authority like God.

~

I think personally, we all have a purpose that we choose. It is not given to us. For me; it's the quest for knowledge; the quest to know the truth. That was drives me to learn. If I can learn one new aspect of a "truth"; then I feel like I have succeeded. I don't think there is an overarching purpose that drives humans. We choose our own path; our own destiny; our own "truth"

~

One Image I have of "my place" in the world is that of a tiny ceramic tile with a particular shape and color. Although I can't see the completed whole, I believe that my piece fits into the very large mural/art that is composed of all living beings. What is mine to do then is to live out the very particularity that is me (following my heart's longings, developing my talents, accepting that I need not/must not conform wholly to external expectations, nor expect others to conform to my expectations). The thorny question, of course, is just how to do that. How do I recognize my heart's longing? What are my talents?

When I am still, I know that I have always felt an inner stirring, a yearning for something "more". Jesus says that the way we know we are the children of God is that our hearts cry out for Abba. That desire, He says, was implanted within us so as to lead us home to God. On a practical level, I try to nourish that longing by contemplative practices, e.g., daily meditation either by myself or with others, by reading about the experiences and counsel of the great mystics, by paying close attention to the natural world (thank you Mary Oliver and David Whyte) often accompanied by our dog on our daily walks (thank you also to our dog who is a master at paying attention to nature). A critical aspect is that my effort is focused more on honoring and sustaining the desire rather than on obtaining a particular result. I can act but not be completely attached to the outcome. Someone said that every person is a message from God as well as a book about God. I believe that and try to deepen my ability to truly listen to what others have to say. Very relevant to this idea is the question about breaking our "bubbles". The more I can know and understand "others" who are different from me, the more I am enriched and can know more about God.

One respondent quoted "be the change you want to see in the world." For me, that speaks to the need to live from the "bottom up" rather than from the "top down". In other words, I don't develop a belief system though logic or accepting solely what I have been taught by authorities, rather I grope through the dim light in my encounters with others, trying to understand what is the most loving way to be with the other. The relationship develops the faith and knowledge rather than the other way around.

I'd like to offer two quotations that really resonate...

"What we choose to fight is so tiny!
What fights with us is so great!
When we win, it's with small things,
And the triumph itself makes us small...
This is how man grows: by being defeated, decisively,
by constantly greater beings." *(Rilke)*

"Fate and freedom are promised to each other. Fate is encountered only by him that actualizes freedom. That I discovered the deed that intends me, that, this movement of my freedom, reveals the mystery to me. But this, too, that I cannot accomplish it the way I intended it, this resistance also reveals the mystery to me. He that forgets all being caused as he decides from the depths, he that puts aside possessions and cloak and steps bare before the countenance - this free human being encounters fate as the counter image of his freedom. It is not his limit but his completion; freedom and fate embrace each other to form meaning; and given meaning, fate - with its eyes, hitherto severe, suddenly full of light - looks like grace itself." (Martin Buber)

I think everyone has their own purpose and it's well worth it to spend a portion of our lives trying to find out what that is and trying to live according to that purpose. I think all the guides out there – religion, meditation, new age guidance, etc. can only provide clues – this really is a solitary path and I think if I take someone else's path, I am almost definitely going in the wrong direction. Right now, I feel like my purpose is to do things that help others, try to calm my unfocused mind, and to try to train my brain to better feel and understand my connection to the world.

⁓

I like the quote that's attributed to the Buddha (although it's also listed in fakebuddhaquotes.com as not attributed to Buddha): "*Your purpose in life is to find your purpose and give your whole heart and soul to it.*"

While on first read, this quote doesn't seem to actually give advice on how to actually "find your purpose" but I think it's contained in the second part - "*give your whole heart and soul to it*" – maybe the act of giving your whole heart and soul to anything – a loved one, a passion, a search, learning, creates purpose and a direction to a meaningful life.

⁓

This project is a really interesting way of finding meaning and connection – instead of examining meaning from an individual perspective, seeing what a group of connected by anonymous people come up with seems like a different and somewhat unique way of looking at a core question of our existence.

⁓

I remember the quote at the end of Monty Python's movie: The Meaning of Life:

"*Try and be nice to people, avoid eating fat, read a good book every now and then, get some walking in, and try and live together in peace and harmony with people of all creeds and nations*".

I think this quote is pretty good – to me I would add trying to make and maintain close relationships and friendships with others.

⁓

Responses to Question 2: What do you think we would find if we were able to completely know one another?

~

We might find insight on why people act/talk the way they do instead of judgement? Walk a mile in their shoes? Understand their point-of-view. Bursting the bubble and completely knowing one another might also cause us to question "The Authorities" we currently believe in. Once we completely know that they are faulty too.

~

What would we find if we were to completely know each other – Such a challenge – who among us is so in tune with themselves that we are able to completely know ourselves, much less others. I don't think we can ever completely know each other. Humans are made up of DNA and experiences, so while there will be basic commonalities of human needs – food, water, clean air, etc. the other parts that make us will drive the wants for power, love, compassion, greed, selflessness, selfishness, etc.

~

I don't know that 'completely' knowing one another is possible, or even if it is the goal. In fact, I don't think that the goal is even necessarily to like one another. I think the goal is to gain an understanding of one another. To understand what motivates one another, what one another care about. I think we would find that we are a lot the same and, in some cases, very different. I think we'd also learn that we are motivated by many of the same things. By understanding each other we can find enough common ground to respect each other and each other's beliefs and boundaries.

~

While I think "completely" knowing each other is not possible in this life, I think it's something we can strive for. At the moment, for me, a good way to do this is to examine every time I feel anger toward someone else or anger in general – there's an opportunity to understand other people better. Every time I dismiss someone or a group of people as "ignorant" – I tell myself that it's not true – or if it is, in other ways, I am just as ignorant. I think if I had perfect understanding of others, I would realize that they aren't "other people" – just different aspects of myself.

~

I found the story of Daryl Davis, an African American musician who reached out to Ku Klux Klansmen to be one of the most inspiring stories I have come across in the last year. See below link to the story in the Washington Post.

https://www.washingtonpost.com/outlook/i-wanted-to-understand-why-racists-hated-me-so-i-befriended-klansmen/2017/09/29

There's also a Netflix documentary on this subject: Accidental Courtesy: Daryl Davis, Race & America. Watch it – an amazing story!

Another suggestion would be the movie "The Florida Project" about a six-year old year living with her Mom in poverty in the "The Magic Castle" motel in Orlando a short distance from Disney Land. Seems like a bummer of a movie but it really good – even funny.

~

Pondering the above question for the past week or so has led me to conclude that we cannot ever completely know one another. There will be a core within each individual that would not be revealed to another person no matter how long nor how deep a relationship is. And, I believe, that this core or essence of a person remains hidden even to its owner much of the time.

To understand another, Person A must enter into her/his inner world. This requires self-study, a high-level energy requirement. Let us say then that Person A steps outside her/his bubble enough and encounters Person B who is similarly inclined to reach out and really "know another person." Only through Person A's self-knowledge is knowledge of Person B practically possible. There are traits they will discover they have in common after routing around in their conversation long enough: Good intentions, fears, anger, boredom, guilt, sorrows, disappointments, desires, goals, empathy, generosity, judgment, probably an inexhaustible list including favorite foods, pastimes, music.

The result of breaking down barriers is that we humans find that we have an awful lot in common with one another, despite obstacles and perceived differences. It does take energy to arrive at this conclusion, and not everyone is willing to commit high-level energy to it. But it is doable, and the result is a feeling of kinship, friendship, and perhaps even love. I think that is what Jesus meant when he said love your neighbor as yourself. Look into another, have a conversation with that person, and you might just wind up being enlightened!

But completely knowing another person? I don't think so. Each of us has way too much invested in "uniqueness." We are perfect in our own imperfection, and, generally, we don't want to fail our own self by revealing imperfection to another. It is a risk, to be judged for each and every part of ourselves. Isn't that what people tend to do, to judge one another? Isn't that why we are in our bubbles to begin with, so that we are not judged by another person's ideas/opinions?

It is often the case that instead of entering into an understanding of another person, there comes a point when Person

A makes no attempt to enter Person B's position, and criticism grows out of the absence of understanding one's own shortcomings. Scottish psychiatrist Maurice Nicoll called this a lack of *"psychological responsibility, both to oneself and to others: a source . . . of the widespread modern unhappiness . . . in which amongst other things, there is a decline in even ordinary human kindness."* (While his observations seem very up-to-the-minute, Nicoll died in 1953.)

~

Breaking down barriers among people in order to understand one another better seems like a great idea to me. But how? I too think leaving one's comfort zone can help. It's true that a lot of folks usually hang out with people who are similar to them. Traveling exposes us to many different kinds of people and is a good way to learn. I think speaking someone's language is very helpful. When some people from Spanish speaking places learn that I can speak their language, I have almost always seen a smile and sometimes a look of pleasant surprise. I think it is very important to maintain an open mind and be respectful when encountering someone different. Even if you really disagree with something they say it does not mean that you must comment. Expressing interest and asking questions I think is conducive to bubble popping. If things get heated stay cool.

Sounds good, right? It's just that that it isn't that easy to do. There are so many factors involved too. If one person approaches another already angry, that's a hard place to start. If dialog turns to name calling, yelling, and/or cutting off each other's sentences it's going to be nearly impossible to reverse. To me one of the most frustrating tactics is to not answer the question. We see politicians do this regularly. And then there is lying and also misinforming. Misinformation can be deliberate or accidental. A slight miscommunication between two people can alter the substance of the subject and be passed to a third and so on. What's that game when people stand in a circle and whisper a sentence, one to the next, full circle and then see how much it changed? Sometimes misinformation is calculated and planned to sway populations. I think another huge factor is one's upbringing. Some are raised and taught to be racist by their parents. Some have been abused, or perhaps experienced some trauma. Maybe someone's parents were teaching them good values, and then at school are exposed to bad ones by peers. I struggle to answer how to pop the bubble when one or both parties comes in with a built-in prejudice. Taking it further, some people sincerely believe in the complete destruction of one group of people and their culture.

Back to "Well, how?". I think the more we can know about different cultures the better we can find similarities. I agree that finding our similarities is the place to start, not the differences. I think that this is challenging to different people to different degrees. I was lucky to have grown up around a diverse mix of people and taught that everyone is really the same and skin color doesn't matter. For someone who's upbringing was the opposite, it's already a bad foundation. So we see things passed down from generation to generation, positive and negative. Sometimes one person can break the chain and take a different path, no longer passing down that baggage. There is also the matter of the cultural traditions and institutionalized beliefs that we are often not even aware of. It's nice to see some of that being talked about more and addressed. I am blessed to live in a place where many cultures overlap. I speak two languages almost daily and have gotten to understand a lot about the other cultures by simply interacting. I think it has been rubbing off on me too. One develops an accent over time. I like it a lot. I can imagine someone who would not.

When I look at the big picture it looks overwhelming and, well, like it will never happen (everyone getting along even if not agreeing). In fact I have my doubts that humanity will change if we haven't throughout history. But why give up? Plus it's fun and interesting! I believe the place to start is with oneself and locally. Go somewhere different and learn. Find the similarities because we love them - they bring smiles and build trust. You can't be friends with everyone and and probably wouldn't want to with some. We don't have to. There's good and bad people of every kind, so logically we should judge one another by character and not color, etc.

~

This is going to be a very pessimistic answer but I believe this will never happen. Since the dawn of man; we have, as a society at large: try to dominate one another. To rule over. To oppress. It is the "survival of the fittest". We; as human beings, are sell centered and only think of our gratifications. Now; that is not everyone. We have countless number of human beings who believe in the greater good. To empathize. To care for others. However; those who have power will always try to retain it and try to demand its will onto others. This could be political; religious, or something else. It is naturally in our DNA. We come from apes and the majority of humans still think in those terms. I would propose that it is unnatural that people empathize and think of others first. I just see the evidence out there today. We are destined to destroy our planet; rape the world resources and make ourselves extinct.

~

Responses to question 3: Do you think there such a thing as a unique, individual "soul"?

~

Yes. But I am open to the possibility of the concept a concept like reincarnation in which the same unique soul might exist in different forms or on different "universes."

~

I believe in the Buddhist philosophy that there is not a unique individual soul. Many other religions contend that there is, but this is too esoteric for me to believe.

~

I would hope to think there is a soul out there with my name on it. They have been thoughts on this in which certain scientists have stated that we are made of Quantum elements and since the Universe is an endless sea of Quantum elements; when person dies; their own "Quanta" selves are preserved and are then brought back to the Universe. Sort of a nice thought. I think people would love to have the ability to "remember" their lives. I pray and hope that is the case.

~

At this point in my life I would say I don't think so. I recently read the following passage from the book "My Antonia" by Willa Cather:

"I was something that lay under the sun and felt it, like the pumpkins, and I did not want to be anything more. I was entirely happy. Perhaps we feel like that when we die and become a part of something entire, whether it is sun and air, or goodness and knowledge. At any rate, that is happiness; to be dissolved into something complete and great. When it comes to one, it comes as naturally as sleep."

That seemed like a really beautiful way of saying that we're a part of something bigger than ourselves – part of everything.

I think life is a temporary state where we think we have egos and don't realize we are an indivisible part of everything else.

~

When I was a kid and went to the Air & Space Museum, there was this video that started with a person's hand and then zoomed into the hand and to the molecular level and then the atomic level and then the subatomic level. The it went in reverse and zoomed out, back to the hand, then the person, the city block, the island of Manhattan, the earth, solar system, galaxy, etc.

Many times I've had the feeling that if we could look our world from the right perspective, we would see "the face of God". Sort of like looking at a painting close up and only seeing paint streaks and then stepping back a few feet to see a masterpiece. That's what I think we are – streaks of paint – by ourselves not important, but as part of a bigger thing, something meaningful.

Responses to question 4: In the Gnostic gospel of Thomas "Jesus said, "Let him who seeks continue seeking until he finds. When he finds, he will become troubled. When he becomes troubled, he will be astonished, and he will rule over the All." Q: What do you think the seeker finds?

OK. This question was enlightening as it caused me to read the Gospel of Thomas, which I had never read. Of course, I can only guess as to his meaning. I think this verse means that an answer is not in and of itself an end.

Each answer gives you more questions. i.e. Gregor Mendel seeks and seeks and finds out the principles of inheritance. But how? Wilhelm Johannsen seeks and seeks and introduces the concept of genes causing inheritance. But what are genes made of? Watson and Crick seek and seek and find out genes are made of DNA. David Comings realizes that most DNA is "junk" (non-coding DNA, the "Dark Matter" of genes). Why have tons of junk DNA? Nessa Carey proposes that this due to epigenetics. Now she seeks to find what causes the DNA to turn off/on. Some DNA turns on during times of famine, some DNA turns on during times of low oxygen etc. Now researchers try to find out how to turn on "good" genes and turn off "bad" genes. When they find the answer to that it will only give us more questions that one can't even think of with the information we currently have. As we go along, we learn to grow better plants and fix various diseases, but each answer creates more difficult questions.

If you go through life thinking you already have all the answers, you never learn. One purpose in life is the process of questioning. I took my friend to see "Book of Mormon." One of the characters, Elder Price, starts off completely, 100% believing everything about his faith. He has no questions; he KNOWS his purpose in life. When life/experiences challenge those beliefs he completely falls apart. He completely loses his purpose in life. (sorry to put 2 Musical Theater references into one month.) But....by the end of the show, Elder Price pulls the good from Mormonism, the good from Star Wars/Star Trek/Tolkien plus the good from outside world and finds a way to help people, give his life purpose and end the show with a Happy Song!

P.S. Verse 114 is interesting: Shimon Kefa says to them: "*Let Mariam depart from among us, for women are not worthy of the life. Yeshua says: Behold, I myself shall inspire her so that I make her male, in order that she also shall become a living spirit like you males. For every female who becomes male, shall enter the Sovereignty of the Heavens.*"

~

Given that I really don't believe in an individual soul, it may seem funny to draw on a soul to answer this question about what the seeker would find. If one continues to seek until they find, then becomes troubled, then astonished, then able to rule over all, I find myself thinking that I probably would find that in the end of the seeking that I discover that I am not who I think I am because I am just a life form while on Earth. I would find that I am an entity of no form, like a soul, and I would be able to rule without motive since my form has been laid bare to nothingness and I am no longer burdened by outer layers. I can rule solely on the betterment of society to the whole world versus particular parties, persons and individual goals.

～

This one is a little over my head, but my question to you is - who said that Jesus answered the quest of the seeker? I glanced through the sayings of the gnostic gospel of Thomas. Some things that caught my attention – the word 'ears' comes up several times in two different contexts. It is used to refer to people who are attempting to come to an understanding of something. As in the phrase 'who has ears hear'. The word 'ears' is also used in reference to seeds which have succeeded in growing. So my theory is that the seeker learned to hear and understand things in a different way than others. That ties back to the bubble question, the goal is not to know everything about one another but rather to understand one another – and one understands through their ears. Understanding what is really at the core of someone, especially someone who is not like you is probably a little troubling until you work on it a little bit. Eventually it gives you the ability find common ground and work towards peace.

And a quick quote sticking with the ear/hearing theme:

"We human beings don't realize how great God is. He has given us an extraordinary brain and a sensitive loving heart. He has blessed

us with two lips to talk and express our feelings, two eyes which see a world of colours and beauty, two feet which walk on the road of life, two hands to work for us, and two ears to hear the words of love. As I found with my ear, no one knows how much power they have in their each and every organ until they lose one."

— Malala Yousafzai

~

I can take this to be "truth". Even if it is not what a person is expecting; the seeker should feel like " the King of the World". To know an absolute "truth"; is something that we need to strive for even if it is against what we feel is the right "truth".

~

First of all, I really don't know, but I thought about it for a while and this is what came to me – I think seeking is a life-long occupation – so I imagine a seeker at the end of his/her life and trying to "figure things out". As he/she does so, they become fearful about dying and question the belief in an after-life, coming to believe that it is a social construct. Once this illusion is dissolved, however, the seeker realizes we're all part of a regenerating universe and also realizes that the illusion of contradictions – insignificant is also infinite, long distances in space and time are actually in the same space and time.

~

Perhaps the seeker will come to the realization, maybe, that true happiness isn't found on earth, but the next best thing is: a sense of purpose that you can share with those that you love.

ROUND 3: *WHAT INSPIRES YOU?*

In November 2018, right before Thanksgiving, I wanted to know what inspires us. Below is my communication and prompt:

I really like the quote by Frank Ostaseski: *"Listening is the shortest distance between two people"* - I look up to all of you and hope to learn from you through this project and look forward to sharing your wisdom with everyone else collaborating on this project, and then ultimately with the rest of the world. But to paraphrase Frank Ostaseki, maybe it's also relevant to say: *"Listening to yourself is the shortest distance to understanding yourself"* - maybe reflecting and responding to these below questions may give you some useful insights.

If inclined, can you consider carving out a half an hour or so from the most hectic time of the year for many of us and help break down the distance between us?

Merry Christmas, Happy Hanakkah, have a festive Festivus and anything else the involves family, friends, or communion. So...

This month's question is....

1. Continuing with the theme of looking for purpose, can you name:
   - One book

- One song
- One piece of art
- One person
- One activity

Responses were reorganized by category and include a few comments not specifically related to the topic of inspiration.

General Observations:

This response deals with purpose in life. For me many universal questions have a theological response. Accordingly, I refer to the writings of Thomas Aquinas (who looks to Augustine, Aristotle and Boethius for guidance.) Human beings must have a purpose, even a vague purpose, or they would never attempt anything. All humans desire some ultimate goal that they think will result in complete satisfaction. I agree with Aquinas in that this ultimate goal is to be found in God alone.

~

Before getting to this month's question regarding purpose, I had some more thoughts on the bubble question. Especially after reading others' responses. I agree that it is not within our capacity to completely know another person's being. We can get to know each other so well that we finish each others' sentences. We can cross barriers in a big scary way, like the story of the black musician reaching out to the Klan. People can have a change of heart and belief. (See La Legende de Saint Julian L'Hospitalier by Flaubert.) The contributor who put forth the statistics about false things people actually believe (pertaining to evolution, climate change, vaccines, etc.) is important to the conversation. There are so many people who hold beliefs that are untrue, preposterous, and maddening. I have a hard time imagining that I would want to even try to understand them. I judge them to be lacking in intelligence and ability to think. This precludes bursting any bubble there. If it is enough that we understand another view even if it disagrees with ours? How can we try to understand it if it is a lie? Even if I understand their motivation, how can I see it as okay (you do your thing, I'll do mine) when it works directly against my wellbeing and others'? The entity attempting to run the country (or ruin it) has worked against bubble bursting without cease since the campaign. How are all these racist, sexist, homophobic, comments allowed to continue? Making fun of disabled people, saying John McCain was not a hero, that Sen. John Lewis (D GA) was all talk and no action. I'm sorry, but fighting for our county and being held a P.O.W. is beyond brave. Being beat by police on the Edmund Pettus Bridge and helping lead the civil rights movement is "all talk"? The problem has been made worse by this rhetoric. We can see the disgusting effects of demagoguery. So, I must ultimately agree with some of the more "negative" entries from last time. There will always be this strife in our nature, and we are headed for self-destruction.

However, in my life I experience some bubble bursting. The other week, I was hanging out in my yard with my Mexican friend. We waved to the Muslim neighbor across the street. I thought to myself, interesting - here I am with two people that have been demonized, threatened to be banned from the country, believed to be rapists and terrorists. But they are no such thing. I don't see a big deal (fortunately for me) in people being different races or religions to burst bubbles with them. Again, to me it comes down to character. Perhaps the many bubbles where I live are very thin and easier to burst. It may be that all of these diverse groups all agree on a few things and thus can coexist, thus sharing one big bubble.

It is interesting and fun to learn about other cultures. Food and music are great islands to find common ground on. What I have a hard time with is people who hold falsehoods as truth. In a conversation we define our terms so we are all on the same page. There is no "definition of terms" so to speak when there is no agreement on basic truths that are proven. Or should I say denial of truth on one side.

In seeking and realizing my purpose there are so many songs, books, works of art, and people that inspire me. For me it comes down to inspiration in general, not one work or person that gave me some unique insight. I am prone to losing faith in humanity, and when I see incredible and great and beautiful things accomplished it gives me hope and makes me want to be excellent too. People can do the best things and the worst things. I try to remember how many good things have been done, built, written, etc. So I see people making the world better, and people making it worse. In keeping with my idea that our collective purpose is to make the world better, I see art, writing, music, food, etc. as all keys to doing this.

My purpose (chosen and instilled) is just a small piece of the collective. It is 1) To try and be a good person to others, and 2) To make and do things I enjoy and feel make the world a little better. Even if it is making a piece of art or furniture, there is still a little more beauty than was in the world before. I like working with things and materials to actualize something I imagine. Others do many other things toward their purpose and helping the world be better through social means. I have great respect for honorable leaders, negotiators, those working toward peace, and anyone who deals with people in their purpose. (oh, yeah, teachers too). I happen to prefer working with plants, metal, wood, stone, etc. Sometimes I fear I am not "helping" the world. Ought I become a mediator for Israel and Palestine? Does it matter? If I am not hurting anyone, isn't that enough? Sometimes I wrestle with this, but ultimately return to the notion that to live a good life is the goal. The activities that I like are gardening and making things. I am able to leave the worldly cares aside and immerse myself in a project. Often they are 10% inspiration and 90% work. The potentially tedious and repetitive tasks can become mediations. I am sanding, sanding, and sanding. I have four or five grits to go through. It is not the "fun" part of the project, but is a necessary journey to take to see the manifestation of the vision.

Another thing I do that I find very rewarding is to repair something for someone. What might be easy for me might seem impossible to them. When they thank me and say this is so much better, I love it. I was able to help someone and got to work with materials and tools. Oh, they even pay me money for it too!

One movie that really affected me since I first saw it as a child, was the one mentioned by one of the contributors. It is called "*Powers of Ten*" and I too saw it at the Air and Space Museum. As it zooms into the hand and then out to the farthest reaches of space, it dives deep to the quantum level and then soars up to the astronomical level. It is truly mind-blowing. Even as a child I thought "What if the Earth is just a particle in an atom in a molecule, making up another word. Are we just an electron? What are we a part of? Another person, planet, dog, car? God?" When I studied Einstein's theories, I learned that the math describing earthly and astronomical events, did not quite work on the atomic level. This echoes the idea that the more we learn, the more we elucidate the mystery.

I like the metaphor of looking at a painting close up and seeing only brush strokes, then moving back to see the whole. I have a similar one (maybe the same); That yes, we are all unique like snowflakes, but when you step back you just see snow. This is how I see people. On the snowflakes level, I can usually find compassion for a unique individual, but looking at the blinding snow of the human collective I feel less so. In the snowstorm of humanity are all the elements of human behavior, positive and negative, but somehow magnified. The "hive" of humans then resembles a behemoth, at once destroying and creating. I get discouraged constantly hearing and seeing the continuation of the negative aspects of our nature, and at the same time inspired by all the positive things that happen. This is hard for me to reconcile. Do I say to our collective "I have no sympathy for your plight, you brought this upon yourself."? Or something like "I am but a small part, but I will try and help if I can." I feel like someone lighting a candle and cursing the darkness at the same time. Perhaps that's how the world will always be, two opposing things coexisting yet each necessary to make the whole? Like negative and positive bonds holding particles together I suspect there must be some need for "bad" in this world. I will echo the quote from another contributor "...you meant it for evil against me, but God meant it for good".

~

This month's challenge is not articulating what gives me insight into how to live my life. The challenge is limiting myself to declaring One book, One song, etc. One. You see, it is nearly impossible to tease out just one of any of these, because the longer life extends, the more bits and pieces of books, songs, artworks, activities and interactions with people I seem to have enfolded into my understanding of life and the world.

~

Although there have been many influences and people important in my seeking for meaning, one person truly shines out. A bit of background...having been raised as a strict Catholic, I encountered many stumbling blocks that left me troubled and anxious, e.g., a focus on obeying rules, adhering to the doctrine that the "truth" could always be referenced by the Baltimore Catechism, a resistance to valuing inner experience, deference to obedience to the hierarchy. Compliance was the goal. (an aside: when I was in college, Catholic college of course, I took a general philosophy class in which the great, enduring questions of the ages were studied. The class looked at how the prominent thinkers and schools of philosophy wrestled with these questions. Then, the professor, a Capuchin monk, would say, "now I'll give you the final answer", which was always the one that Thomas of Aquinas advocated. Naive as I was, even then I could see the folly of anyone having all the definitive answers.)

One day, while I was in my thirties, I noticed in the paper a picture of an Episcopal priest who was gathering an ecumenical group of prayerful people who were going to explore eastern spirituality and its relevance to western spirituality. They were planning a weekend retreat nearby and I, very uncharacteristically, acted on what felt like a whim and signed up. The weekend was a life-transforming experience and introduced me to contemplative prayer and nondual thinking and perceiving. I also met someone there, Jerry May of Shalem Institute, who became the most influential person in my spiritual life for the next decades. His nonjudgmental acceptance of all that is, his focus on desire itself (the desire for love, truth, God) as the way, his trust in the dark night, his belief that we are led by our hearts toward the One Who created our hearts....I could go on, but I think this gives a general picture. When he died, his last word was "trust".

~

Books

Books that have deep meaning for me over the course of time include *Being Peace* by Thich Nhat Hanh. He is a Buddhist monk, originally from Vietnam. He writes convincingly about the true self and finding the true self, which then is fully capable of compassion and peace. As a peace activist, he was nominated for the Nobel Peace Prize by none other than Martin Luther King, Jr. I am all about peace and harmony. *The Guide* Maimonides lived in the 1100s. *for the Perplexed* by Moses Maimonides, is a logical book that lays down some foundational thoughts. This book clarifies so much for people exploring Judeo-Christian thought. He is considered to be a great Jewish philosopher because of his contribution to science and religion. Consider that he said our very thoughts and words originated with God. That gives one plenty to ponder.

The Last Temptation of Christ by Nikos Kazantzakis. This author of *The Fratricides* and *Zorba the Greek* was also a gifted philosopher. In fact, his body of work is in its totality compelling reading.

To Kill a Mockingbird still stands the test of time for me. I was in elementary school when the movie was released and I remember being mesmerized by the court scenes and Scout's interaction with Bo. As I got older, I read the book and saw the movie again and again. Having relatives from the deep South who lived in a town remarkably like the town in the book, I began questioning how people came to see other human beings as less human than they were just because of the color of their skin. Later, this questioning expanded to religious, physical, sexual, ethnic, etc. differences. I was determined to evaluate people on my interaction with them and not on visual aspects of their person.

I really liked *A Brief History of Time* by Steven Hawking. It was the first book I remember reading about the "Big Questions"

One book - *Return to Love*, Marianne Williamson

I would pick *The Fountainhead*, by Ayn Rand, profoundly influenced me in my early adulthood and helped shape my political views. The protagonist, Howard Roark, represents the spirit of individualism. Ayn Rand's views and later, Barry Goldwater, helped shape my belief that government intervention in our lives and social systems, on balance, and despite good intention, tends to corrupt our social structures.

My book nominee would be *The Goldfinch* by Donna Tartt. It may seem like an odd choice for "meaning of life issues," but it is peppered with great insights into living.

The book *Touching the Void: The True Story of One Man's Miraculous Survival* by Joe Simpson provides a reminder to me of human beings' incredible resiliency and ability to overcome obstacles. I try to apply this story to everyday life and try to power on despite sometimes minor things that can derail us from achieving our goals.

I nominate *To Kill a Mockingbird* because it speaks to doing the right thing in spite of immense social pressure to do otherwise.

The *Harry Potter* books captured my imagination as a child. What an amazing vision J. K. Rowling had and what amazing obstacles she faced and surmounted to create her vision.

Music

To me, *Hallelujah*, written by Leonard Cohen, is almost the perfect song – from a lyrical standpoint, it covers all of the key themes of our existence – trying to understand our purpose, our relationships to others, relationship to God, rebellion from God, sex, loneliness, desire for connection. The chord structure is very simple and is described in the song – "*It goes like this, the fourth, the fifth. The minor fall, the major lift. The baffled king composing hallelujah*". My favorite verse is the sixth. To me, it makes me think about Adam or Eve having a (probably) one-way conversation with God after he has expelled them from the garden of Eden.

You say I took the name in vain
I don't even know the name
But if I did, well really, what's it to you?
There's a blaze of light in every word
It doesn't matter which you heard
The holy or the broken hallelujah

Cohen has said of the song's meaning: *"It explains that many kinds of hallelujahs do exist, and all the perfect and broken hallelujahs have equal value."* I interpret this to mean that there's different paths to knowledge. Anyway, it's one thing to write about the song – go listen to it carefully – it's an amazing and inspirational song.

Music is a special love. It is impossible to select just one song that gives me insight into how to live my life. So I will say Johann Sebastian Bach is at the top of my list of musical geniuses; every piece of his is stirring and inspires me. But, on a more pedestrian plane, I love *The New Century Hymnal*, used in the United Church of Christ (and perhaps other denominations) for worship. It interprets the Holy Bible – the very best book of all time for guiding one through life and into deep relationship with God – in song and psalters. Singing two or three hymns on Sunday is joyful; to have their tunes and words humming through my brain all week through is always moving in the most mundane and sublime ways.

My favorite song is *Golden* by Jill Scott, an inspiring song about empowerment and living "in the flow"

I'm taking my own freedom
Putting it in my song
Singing loud and strong

Grooving all day long
I'm taking my freedom
Putting it in my stroll
I'll be high-steppin' y'all
Letting the joy unfold

I am moved by the song: "*Go on ahead and go home*" (Iris Dement) which speaks of redemption and connection to "the ancient ones":

"*In the deep of the night, In the deep of the night*
By the river so still where sorrows come to heal
And wrongs are made right
Down in the deep of the night, In the deep of the night
On a creaking porch swing, the ancient ones sing
"everything is alright"

One song – *You've Got a Friend* by Carol King inspires me – The lyrics can be interpreted in many ways and for most people the "friend" is God. I interpreted it that the "friend" is the person inside of you who is always there for you and from where you can draw strength even when you feel all alone. Each person has an immense amount of resiliency if they only believe in themselves and seek what should be the love and acceptance of oneself. (*Note: Carol King has stated that "the song was as close to pure inspiration as I've ever experienced. The song wrote itself. It was written by something outside myself, through me."*)

I think the song: *I Wish I Knew How It Would Feel To Be Free* (composed by Billy Taylor and sung by Nina Simone) is sort of what this project is trying to accomplish:

"*I wish I could share*
All the love that's in my heart

Remove all the bars
That keep us apart
I wish you could know
What it means to be me
Then you'd see and agree
That every man should be free"

I love Handel's Messiah – it's one of the things I look forward to at Christmas mass. Handel's Messiah is an oratorio, which is a large musical composition for orchestra, choir, and soloists. This work is comprised of three parts – the first part starts with the Old Testament foretelling the coming of Christ and includes the Birth of Jesus. Part two includes the passion of Christ, his crucifixion, resurrection and ascension. The last part includes the Jesus's promise of redemption for us all and the second coming of Christ and victory of good over evil. The whole of my religion pared with the most sublime musical accompaniment.

I heard about Eva Cassidy's version of *Over the Rainbow* before I first heard it probably in 2001. I read something about a British DJ who had discovered the song and her music five years after her death in 1996 and was obsessed with her voice. The song was included in her posthumously-released compilation album "Songbird", released in 1998 and was released as a CD single in 2001. In particular, I like the point at 3:30 minute mark of the song when she shifts from her understated version to the full range of the emotion of her voice. What a voice! I wish I could have seen her perform at the Blues Alley in Georgetown or somewhere else.

The song *Gimme Shelter* is an apocalyptic song about murder, rape, a flood, and a storm that is *"threatening my very life today"*. The frequently repeating refrain is: *"It's just a shot away"*. Despite this, song ends with a revised refrain: *"I tell you love, sister, It's just a kiss away. It's just a kiss away."* (repeated five more times). It's a terrifying, ominous song but with just a possible note of optimism at the end.

My favorite song is Stephen Foster's *Beautiful Dreamer*. The first published version of this song states that is was: *"the last song ever written by Stephen C. Foster. Composed but a few days prior to his death."* Here's a beautiful stanza:

Beautiful dreamer, out on the sea
Mermaids are chanting the wild Lorelei
Over the streamlet vapors are borne
Waiting to fade at the bright coming morn

My favorite song is *Amazing Grace*. This song was written in 1772 by the English poet and clergyman John Newton. Interestingly, this song, which has prominently associated with the civil rights movement was written by a man involved in the slave trade prior to his conversion to Christianity. If you want to listen to this song on a music streaming service, check out Mahalia Jackson's version – enough said!

The song *Changes in Latitude* by Jimmy Buffett is meaningful to me because it speaks to finding the humor in every situation and focusing on the future and not the past:

It's those changes in latitudes,
changes in attitudes nothing remains quite the same.
With all of our running and all of our cunning,
If we couldn't laugh, we would all go insane.

Speaking of Jimmy Buffett, did you know he has a younger brother? His name is "All you can eat" (that's a joke – "All you can eat Buffet").

I like the song: "*Dreams*" by Fleetwood Mac. It's a melancholy song about a breakup, but the song and lyrics are mystical and haunting:

Now here I go again, I see the crystal visions
I keep my visions to myself, it's only me
Who wants to wrap around your dreams and,
Have you any dreams you'd like to sell?

Art

There are too many stellar pieces of art. As a fine artist, I can say only that Albrecht Durer, Leonardo DaVinci and Michelangelo hold my interest longer than any other artist's work. But then there are Boticelli, Grandma Moses and many contemporary botanical artists such as Jean Emmons and Elaine Searle. Creating art is one of highest endeavors of human beings and brilliant masters teach much through their art. Why else do people study the Mona Lisa's visage centuries after she was painted?

A painting that is a source inspiration for me is a painting of my Mom's that she made for me. She combined three concepts together for me – an Ouroboros (a snake eating its tail), the physicist Roger Penrose's idea of "three worlds and three mysteries" – the physical world, consciousness, and mathematical forms and the mystery about how these three worlds create and relate to each other. The third "reference" is the background of the painting – the universe depicted in a manner similar to the cover art of *God's Debris* by Scott Adams (the "Dilbert" cartoonist), a book that conveyed the concept that the pantheistic concept that the universe itself is God, who gave up his omnipotence and omniscience in order to experience physical reality and that the unfolding of the universe is the action of recreating him/her self. Anyway, I am blown away by an artist's ability to convey separate ideas/concepts into one beautiful, meaningful piece of art.

One piece of art – *The David* by Michelangelo – this was a difficult category since the breadth of great art is endless. I am fascinated with the complexity and skill needed to sculpt such a real image of a human being in such a giant masterpiece. Every muscle and nuance told a story of the strength of the person being sculpted.

Van Gogh's *Starry Night* because it speaks to how everybody sees things just a little bit differently

I am attracted to artistic photographs of landscapes

The art of the Sistine Chapel is the most amazing work of art from, in my opinion, our greatest artist, Michelangelo

My favorite is *Guernica* by Pablo Picasso

I think Disney's *Peter Pan* animated movie is a beautiful work of art evoking the sense of our lost innocence of childhood, desire to fly, and love of fairy tales where good prevails over evil.

One piece of art: my wife is an amazing painter. There's one painting of her uncle, who was a Monsignor. This painting hangs on the stairs to our second floor. To me, that painting captures the man – his sense of humor, his love of life, and his religious reverence.

The painting *The Isle of the Dead* by Arnold Bocklin has always beguiled me. Every time I am in Manhattan, I try to visit the Metropolitan Museum of Art to view this painting. The painting is a small island with a steep rock circling about two thirds of the island. A small boat what appears to me to be white statue of a woman in front and an oarsman in back and is approaching the island. This painting conveys both a sense of dread as well as a sense of beauty. The statue or figure in the front of the boat reminds me of the Adams Memorial sculpture (also known as "Grief") by Augustus Saint-Gaudens, which is another source of inspiration. I also like the name the sculptor gave to it – "*The Mystery of the Hereafter and The Peace of God that Passeth Understanding*".

A Person

People who are a guiding force for the life journey are many, many loved ones. Singling any one out is too tempting and also too difficult; depending where one is on life's journey a different person is more helpful than another.

One person – the list of great people is also long, but I decided to select someone in my lifetime who made it his life's work to bring joy to families – Walt Disney. I grew up with Disney (pre-parks, of course) and remember the entire family gathering around the TV with our popcorn to watch Disney once a week. The stories were simple, heart-warming, usually with a lesson involved and could be watched by the entire family. We laughed together and enjoyed the simplicity of family coming together. Of course, the popcorn was a bid draw, too.

Allen White is the minister of my church and one of my very good friends, he is also the author of the book "God is All". He inspires me because he lives strictly according to his faith in God. He believes God is All, truly all, so he relies on nothing but his faith and deals with all challenges through prayer – meditation. So, when most people will think about what action to take to address a challenge, his thing is to get still and listen. His common statement, is that all things can be taken care of through time in the prayer closet – meditation.

One person I really admired was Father Lorenzo Albacete – he was a priest at St John the Evangelist for a number of years. I remember him once speaking about faith – he described it basically as a choice. No one knows if there is a God or a purpose. We have to make a decision how we want to live. To him it's a choice between hope, wonder, and a map for how to live your life versus despair and hopelessness. To him it was an easy choice. That's pretty much how I feel. The other thing I liked about Father Albacete was his irreverence sense of humor. He would curse on the altar and tell jokes. Mass for him was not a solemn rite but rather a celebration. He was trained as a physicist and viewed science with wonder and joy. He wrote a book: *Attraction to Infinity* which captures his intelligence, passion, awe, and sense of humor.

I would pick Alexander Hamilton for his amazing contributions to democracy.

Galileo - He, to me, was the first one who really opened the window to the universe and was then persecuted for it

This is always changing but I just read Malala's book and I am currently very inspired by her ability to not let hate into her heart despite being attacked with such hate. She is the literal definition of the Christian sentiment of turning the other cheek.

One person who comes to mind is Wangari Maathai, the Kenyan environmentalist and human rights activist. I met her in 1994 at her home/compound in the outskirts of Nairobi. I didn't really know too much about her at the time except that I knew she couldn't leave her compound because she would be arrested. Her compound was a collection of stray animals and people who didn't have anywhere else to live. I was struck by her gentleness, her humbleness, and overall "presence". in 2004, she became the first African woman to receive the Nobel Prize for her "her contribution to sustainable development, democracy and peace." If you want to learn more about her, I think her autobiography *Unbowed, a Memoir* is terrific.

As a child, I loved Steve Irwin and his TV show: "*The Crocodile Hunter*". I loved his passion for what he did, his sense of humor, ability to entertain and teach at the same time. I think he inspired many kids to learn and to explore. He should be a model for all teachers. I remember the day he died. I was crushed.

Activity

One activity – always it is being able to help someone. Who doesn't feel better than after they can do something for someone else. Making that time should be more of a priority for me. It is something for me to continue to strive to do.

I feel at my best when I am exercising and listening to a good podcast

Meditation

I'll say it is three activities: doing good things for other people (for in giving do we receive much); walking or hiking (communing with Nature is a sure antidote for a lot that is otherwise wrong in the world); and painting (it is very Zen and that leads me directly to my inner self and back out again as I put myself on paper or vellum).

One activity: For many years, I have enjoyed the poetry of Kahlil Gibran. I was attracted to the mysticism and message of love and universality of religion. Here's a line I like:

"*You are my brother and I love you. I love you when you prostrate yourself in your mosque and kneel in your church and pray in your synagogue. You and I are sons of one faith—the Spirit.*"

Charity work is really valuable because it always gives you perspective on how lucky you really are.

I love to play the piano. It's amazing how playing makes me feel good and calms me.

The times I feel "transcended" is listening to live music by a great performer – for me some of those performers have been

Iris Dement, Alison Kraus, Emmy the Great, Sierra Hull, Dry Branch Fire Squad, and Billy Joe Shaver.

My favorite activity is travel—because it opens us up to the world. Here's a quote for you by Ray Bradbury: "*Stuff your eyes with wonder, live as if you'd drop dead in ten seconds. See the world. It's more fantastic than any dream made or paid for in factories.*"

My favorite activity is sitting at the beach – it's the one place where your senses are so positively impacted- sight, smell, sound, touch.

I like poetry, especially poetry that conveys life lessons. My favorite is *If* by Rudyard Kipling. I particularly like the following stanza which talks about achieving balance in your life:

If you can dream—and not make dreams your master;
If you can think—and not make thoughts your aim;
If you can meet with Triumph and Disaster
And treat those two impostors just the same

ROUND 4: *WHAT IS THE BIG SLEEP?*

We continued our project with this communication on January 1st, 2018:

Now that we have had our egg nog and champagne and find ourselves in the heart of winter and starting the new year, let's get back to tackling the big questions - this time I ask you to think and share about death and regeneration.

So to set up the topic, let's start with Bruce:

Well now everything dies baby that's a fact
But maybe everything that dies someday comes back
Put your makeup on, fix your hair up pretty
And meet me tonight in Atlantic City.

(Atlantic City - Bruce Springsteen)

So, without any specific questions, I ask you to share your thoughts on the topic of death and how it should guide us in how we live our life.

Here are some prompts, but I emphasize that these only suggestions to stimulate thought - some of the most interesting responses have deviated from the "script" so feel free to go where you will with this (note some of these prompts are taken or modified from questions provided when we started the project.)

- is there a purpose to death? If so what?

- why does it oftentimes have to be so unpleasant, painful, and sad?
- are the answers provided by religion and other belief systems ways to avoid the hard truth that "death brings non-existence"?
- is physical death a metaphor for the immediacy of life? - or to quote Norman Cousins: *"Death is not the greatest loss in life. The greatest loss is what dies inside us while we live."*
- is the purpose of life closely tied to the reality of death?

Now you might think this is not the cheeriest topic to bring in the new year, but years ago someone told me that they thought the purpose of life was to try to figure things out, try to make the world a better place, laugh a lot, and leave the world with a sense of peace. That makes sense to me but I think leaving this world with a sense of peace takes a life of effort.

So let›s do it! I›ll leave with one more quote that I hope will inspire you with a sense of urgency from the song *Ain't Wastin' No More Time* by Gregg Allman:

With the help of God and true friends, I've come to realize
I still have two strong legs, and even wings to fly
So I ain't a-wastin time no more
'Cause time goes by like pouring rain, and much faster things

~

While I believe in the existence of God (life appears too complex to have just developed from evolution alone), I view God as getting things started but then letting the world run on its own (why there is so much death, killings, war, etc). Accordingly, I then view death as a way to permit the system to run. If we didn't die, we'd have overpopulation, which would cause death anyways. To me it is much more logical that biological parts would wear out with time. Medicine has countered some of that, but I don't think we will see a full reversal of it in our lifetimes (if ever).

So, despite religion talking about an afterlife of some sorts, I don't believe in it. I believe that when you're dead, all is gone. Your spirit may survive in your survivors, but only because they keep the thought of you alive. To me it is very understandable why most religions talk about an afterlife. What a great way to encourage people to behave!

To the extent that death takes place because parts wear out (disease, old age, etc), it is not surprising that it is painful or awkward. We all desire to continue living and, therefore, resist dying. I have known a few people who wanted to die and did so quickly (my grandfather, who after he determined that his wife of 70 years was really dead, just stopped eating and died in a couple of days). Few of us would be happy with euthanasia, given the risk of mischief.

~

Interesting question. I do believe, as Bruce's song says, that "*everything that dies someday comes back.*" And I believe truly in an joyful "afterlife." As C.S. Lewis says "*Joy is the serious business of heaven.*" I do think "heaven" is a new step of existence that we can't even comprehend. But I do think Love lasts. The purpose of death is to get to that spot. Because of telomeres and other physical issues, much of your purpose in life is stolen as you become disabled by age and you need to go to the next level. The main purpose of religion (in addition to offer guidance on how to live and provide a supportive community) is to help us become comfortable with the concept of death. That is one reason why Jesus had to die.

At an interview a few years ago, I was asked "*Have you made your peace with death?*" because the population I would be working with always dies within 6 months to a year. As Bruce's song says: "*everything dies baby that's a fact*" and if I was going to fall apart every time someone died, I would be useless to them. Immediately, without thinking, said "Yes." I truly felt I had "made my peace" with death.

I started working with dying people when I was young and I started with a group of "girls" about my age. We have sometimes wondered if being so comfortable with death so young skewed our perspective on life? At the height of the HIV epidemic, we took care of young dying guy after young dying guy. To me, death is as natural a part of life as birth. And a lot (most?) of the misery of death comes from the often ridiculous fight our medical community puts up against death. And I think that is because, as a culture, we are not comfortable with death.

We are one of the first generations where we are not exposed to death early in life. Back when 50+% of kids died before age 5, everyone dealt with death as kids. Family members were laid out on the dining room table. Perhaps some of the drop in participation in religious rituals in the western world may stem from the fact that most people do not have to deal with death until they are adults?

With HIV and cancer, death often seems like a Huge Relief. I took a Death and Dying graduate level class and wrote that I didn't fear death, but I did fear the dying process.

But it is funny you ask it this way, because over the summer I had a several day-stretch waiting on a biopsy. And I was surprised at how stressful it was. If I truly was "at peace" with death, I thought I would have been more pragmatic. It made me question the validity of my belief system.

Everything came back OK. (thank goodness) but afterwards I told my spouse that I was really, truly surprised at how much I had stress I experienced. I thought when my time came (which happily hadn't yet) I would be totally cool with it.

As I thought about it afterward, it seemed like one should be stressed/upset. If one were not sad at impending death, it would indicate a lack of appreciation of the joy beauty of life.

When his wife died, CS Lewis wrote *"The pain now is part of the happiness then. That's the deal."*

He wrote books called *The Problem of Pain, Surprised by Joy,* and *A Grief Observed* which dealt with death and suffering within a Christian perspective. This was partially the basis of the movie Shadowlands. (A really good movie except that CS Lewis was played by Anthony Hopkins so I kept expecting him to eat Debra Winger's face- it was right after Silence of the Lambs)

That Norman Cousins' quote is really good, and quite true. It is not a tragedy if someone dies, it is a tragedy if they feel forced to violate their belief system!

⌐

Rumination about death

When we were young, death seemed oh so far away as to be nearly nonexistent. We thought we might go on living forever and there was always tomorrow. Yes, pets, bugs, plants died, but usually not people until they were old.

When I was 8 or 9 years old, I was visiting with cousins and their cousins at their family home, which also was a funeral home. We were running around and playing some game, when wow, I ran into the funeral parlor itself. There was a body laid out for viewing, although there was no visiting hour then—

what a surprise to my young eyes. As I was alone, I stopped in mid-step to check out the deceased. My first dead body. So I guess I started thinking about death itself at that point, because I had seen it for myself.

It wasn't a frequent topic in our household and there were not that many deaths to discuss. I came to think of death as a state of becoming eternally silent. Somewhere around eighth grade I remember thinking that if I lived to be 56 years old that would be a fine age to die. I would have accomplished some good things in life and would know my grandchildren. That seemed sufficient until I was somewhere in my teens, when all of us become much more aware of the big events in life and their meaning on personal and grand scales. Religious learning was begun in earnest, and I have never stopped exploring questions/answers from a philosophical, existential, or theological standpoint.

For many people, I think, there is genuine fear not so much of death, but of the process of dying itself. The physical pain and the pain of separating from people and life as we know it and all that entails. I imagine some of the recent books on this topic are eloquent (When Breath Becomes Air, for example). I have not read them yet.

Would we live a different life if we were to somehow know when we will die? Perhaps. For sure, people would have a great sense of urgency in the "do it now, don't wait" approach to life. More powerful a question might be: What if you thought you might be at death's threshold, and then recover? How would you then live your life? There have been many people who have related their near-death or out-of-body experiences. I believe that such reports are not made up exactly, though it is difficult to describe an otherworldly event in human terms. I had an out-of-body experience during a serious illness many years ago that changed my worldview and influenced countless life choices ever since. Foremost I learned then and there that conversation with God is welcome and possible. Second, there is life after life as we know it, but we cannot know its nature from this side. Third, there should be no fear. It can be replaced with faith and love. (I use the word "should" here, but have sworn off using it, because it implies "I know better" and I really don't.)

Because of that experience, I approach life with a bit more joie de vivre. I truly believe that we are meant to be happy and not fearful. (That doesn't mean that I do not worry sometimes needlessly.) It led me to deeper faith in God and Jesus Christ, not just from my upbringing, religious journey, or philosophical underpinnings, but because I was enlightened in that experience. Literally.

Life as we know it is finite in death. There is always more of God's truth to be revealed, and it must be on "the other side" that God's truth is discerned. Meeting God face to face: can anyone imagine anything akin to that?

In our daily lives we glimpse our blessings. There are unknown blessings, too, that we cannot see. This is the ultimate blessing: In death, we will return to our Creator. Of course, we are made of the same stuff as the stars (a statement some other respondent made in an earlier round in *What Have We Learned So Far*, and is true) but just think: We will meet the great I Am who created the stars and us. Will we be reunited with our parents or other loved ones? What about meeting George Washington or Martin Luther King, Jr.? Wow. The possibilities are endless and in our human and limited understanding, priceless.

While I love philosophical writings on this topic of death/life, many decades of thinking and reading have led me to desire ever more peace and harmony, joy and love in my life. I probably have not answered the probing questions very deeply here as listed in the email from Paul, but these comprise the essence of the life that I choose to live. It was a blessing that much was shown to me in my out-of-body experience, for I saw with great clarity what was important and have followed that path as much as possible ever since.

Just another take on this topic is this opening of a great old song from Blood, Sweat and Tears:

I'm not scared of dying
And I don't really care
If it's peace you find in dying
Well, then let the time be near

If it's peace you find in dying
And if dying time is here just bundle up my coffin
'Cause it's cold way down there
I hear that it's cold way down there
Yeah, crazy cold way down there

And when I die, and when I'm gone
There'll be one child born
In this world to carry on, to carry on

There have been innumerable words written on death, in the scriptures, by poets, authors, and many others. All that is well said better by those people. Let me focus on something that has resonated with me over the years.

In our lives we focus on ourselves, careers, the pursuit of goals, wealth and the like. It is easy to lose sight of the unseen, the unimagined, the real purpose of us breathing air. In the movie Gladiator, Maximus Decimus Meridius tells his soldiers: "*What we do in life echoes through eternity.*" To me the quote states a fundamental truth with a Biblical flavor: Life is brief, eternity is unending, our lives matter in eternity.

For the sake of brevity, I think there is a very practical way to keep these thoughts in our minds. Visit a cemetery! I have heard clerics speaking on this topic.

We all spend our lives trying to avoid the topic, but death is inevitable. Visiting a cemetery affords us the chance to reflect on our lives and to focus our minds on what really matters in our march to the grave.

You'll be able to ask yourself hard questions. Am I being a good enough person, father, mother? Is this the year I give priority to what really matters to someone like me who is briefly drawing breath on this planet?

Your life has meaning and purpose. And some day it will end. The cemetery will remind you of that. But it will also give you clarity and focus.

⁓

Before offering my own thoughts on death and life, I'd like to share John O'Donahue's words:

"Every human person is inevitably involved with two worlds: the world they carry within them and the world that is out there. All thinking, all writing, all action, all creation and all destruction is about that bridge between the two worlds. All thought is about putting a face on experience. One of the most exciting and energetic forms of thought is the question. I always think that the question is like a lantern. It illuminates new landscapes and new areas as it moves. Therefor, the question always assumes that there are many different dimensions to a thought that you are either blind to or that are not available to you. So a question is really one of the forms in which wonder expresses itself. One of the reasons that we wonder is because we are limited, and that limitation is one of the great gateways to wonder.

All thinking that is imbues with wonder is graceful and gracious thinking. And thought, if it's not open to wonder, can be limiting, destructive and very, very dangerous.

One of the sad things today is that so many people are frightened by the wonder of their own presence. They are dying to tie themselves into a system, a role, or to an image, or to a predetermined identity that other people have actually settled on for them. This identity may be totally at variance with the wild energies that are rising inside in their souls. Many of us get very afraid and we eventually compromise. We settle for something that is safe, rather than engaging the danger and the wildness that is in our own hearts."

And so, I approach the topic of death in an attitude of wonder. As far as I know, there's been no scientifically proven instance of someone coming back from the dead to tell us about it. There must be a reason for that, but I sure don't know what it is. Science doesn't give a definitive answer. Religions try, but....? However, despite not being "sure", there are some things I have come to believe about death. One is that it's safe. It's not the end but rather a transition to some new awareness/consciousness/love. I believe that, somehow, after death, we rejoin the great Being from which we came. Of course, a huge question here is why we experience this fleeting moment of human existence at all? What is needed from us in our human lives? I suspect that the answer may have something to do with being given a chance to be co-creators of the material world, that through love we can add our own energetic spark to existence. In an earlier offering, I had shared an image of each person being a tiny tile that ultimately will form a divine mosaic. If so, then my life here is to actualize that tile, to become the particularity that is me.

Recently, a friend told me that she had purchased a burial plot at Holy Cross Abbey in Virginia (a beautiful and hospitable place where I have gone on personal retreats). The monks tend to the graves and unembalmed bodies or ashes can only be enclosed in plain wooden boxes. That struck me as being both sensible and holy; I recoil from the big business model of burial that starts with embalmment and continues with an armored casket. That seems to imply that death is the enemy that we need to defend against.

Still, I have so many questions. But as O'Donahue says, the question can become a lantern that illuminates new landscapes. I look forward to the exploration!

A final quote. St. Clare of Assisi is reported to have said on her deathbed, *"thank you, God, for letting me be a human."*

~

At this point in my life, the topic of death is more just a scary thought to me right now as the parent with kids who are so young and dependent on me and my spouse. I would never want them to have to deal with the loss of a loved one at such a young age, as I think it would really change the trajectory of their lives. And I want them to be raised a certain way, and there is no guarantee of that if we aren't there to ensure it. Probably the most I have thought about it recently is to just make sure I am living in the moment and enjoying the time I do have here with my family. They are the most important thing, and the inevitability and unpredictability of death makes life and all moments and memories we make all the more precious.

The Facebook post by Holly Butcher, shortly after her death at the age of 27 captures my views on the topic - death is a reminder to live your life to the fullest, help those around us, and spend time wisely with our family and friends. One of my favorite quotes from the post is:

"Give, give, give. It is true that you gain more happiness doing things for others than doing them for yourself. I wish I did this more. Since I have been sick, I have met the most incredibly giving and kind people and been the receiver of the most thoughtful and loving words and support from my family, friends and strangers; More than I could I ever give in return. I will never forget this and will be forever grateful to all of these people."

Check out the full post at: http://people.com/human-interest/dying-australian-woman-leaves-note-goes-viral/

~

My belief on what happens after death is that it is unknowable. So I have limited interest in opinions on what comes after. If someone claims knowledge like a religion, I view them as scammers. If an individual makes a claim of knowledge, then I believe them to be delusional or lying. I do believe living as if you will be judged is a good rule to follow. Pursuing a life of morality leads to a more fulfilling life for you and your loved ones. And of course, if there is a judgement you will be prepared.

~

Is there a purpose to death? Is physical death a metaphor for the immediacy of life? Is the purpose of life closely tied to the reality of life? On a tombstone, there are usually beginning and ending life dates, with a hyphen in between representing the summary of a person's life on earth. I was once told, it is not these dates are important, but what you do with the hyphen between these dates. Knowing that death is inevitable, it is important to use your time on earth wisely. This is a lofty goal since no one knows when their own death will occur and most of us allow the trivialities of life to interfere with making the most of living. The attitude is that there is always a tomorrow to regain focus on what matters most. Unfortunately, an accident, another person's death, a traumatic event, our own aging are the most common wake-up moments to begin to focus on the remainder of our lives. However, that said, we are all human and this seems to be a common human trait, so it is the rare human that can refocus early to make the most of their time on Earth. So, the purpose of death to me, is to remind me to live life in the moment as best one can. I agree with Norman Cousins that Death is not the greatest loss in life, but the greatest loss is what dies inside us while we live.

Why is death so often unpleasant, sad or painful? – I do not tie death to "God's plan for being alive". I believe death is a function of the human body (other than accidental deaths) and science. There are so many components to a body and brain that it is amazing to me that we exist as long as we do given how much we tend to abuse our body during our lifetime. I also think that so much of the pain, etc. is self-made. We seem determined to make our loved ones use all the medical treatments available to keep someone alive for a short time in a state of living that is physically painful or mentally debilitating with limited to zero quality of life just to have them around for our needs, not theirs. I believe I or my family should be allowed to assist me along in death when the quality of life is more painful that the thought of living. I don't want society making that choice for me. I also find it interesting that people who have such a strong faith that heaven is the ultimate goal tend to take extreme measures to stay in the Earthly world.

Does religion and other belief systems avoid the hard truth that death brings non-existence? I was raised by one parent, my Dad, who did not have religious beliefs and thus believed that when he died that was it. My Mom, on the other hand, had complete faith in her Catholic religion and believed that death brought complete peace. Going through lingering deaths with both my parents was interesting. My Dad and I had much chance to talk about death and he lamented that it would be so much easier if he had Mom's faith and could draw comfort from death. Mom's faith, as she slowly marched towards death never changed. I was able to ask both Mom and her sister prior to any illnesses what they thought death was like since they both had such a strong Catholic faith and they answered in the same way – death brought eternal peace.

Neither of my parents feared death, but for completely different reasons. Dad wanted death to take him because he was in a diminished capacity and this was humiliating for him as he was such a larger than life presence on Earth. To be dependent on someone for every bodily need was too much for him to bare. Mom, was stoic about her demise and did wonder why God did not take her sooner since she no longer saw a need for living (this also was a remark that her sister made to me during her own last illness when Mom was not around), but Mom never lost the faith that God would eventually come. For me, another nonbeliever, I was surprisingly distraught knowing Dad believed in only the finality of death, while Mom gave me comfort through her strong faith that she knew death would bring her eternal peace. I find my reaction interesting.

~

I am guessing that my opinions and perspective of death is going to vastly different than most. I view death as the end, nothing is after death. Death is exactly as it appears. I do not have visions of eternal existence post death. I believe that the notion of life after death is a social construct to help make sense of loss or false hope of something better beyond. A person ceases to be at death. Everything just stops. Having said that, I am not as fearful of death as you would think. I accept that that is the natural completion of the cycle of life. All living things began and all living things will end. I know this sound incredibly depressing, but to the contrary, it makes every day a celebration that I am still here. I value my time existing and try to make the best of the opportunities given via life. A curious outcome of this belief is that I will never know that I died.

~

This one is a little heavy for my taste but I'll play along anyway.

My theory is that we shouldn't focus on death any more than is helpful in maximizing our living of life. According to lore, Elvis Presley wore a Christian cross pendent and he also wore a pendant with the Hebrew word/symbol Chai on it. When asked why as a Christian, he wore a 'Jewish' symbol, he said he didn't want to miss out on heaven on a technicality. It's interesting that Elvis's heaven safeguard was the symbol Chai which is the Hebrew word for life.

Are religion's answers really just avoiding a hard truth? Maybe, but so what. If living a kinder, less selfish life in the hopes of going to heaven leads to you actually leading a kinder better life. That is a good thing. If having a faith belief in a heaven or afterlife offers comfort to something that you are powerless to control or change, that is also a good thing too. We don't really know what purpose death has, or if there is an afterlife as religion suggests. I think not knowing is meant to be life's great mystery. In the immortal words of Jimmy Buffett (who we can learn from in most life situations): *"Searching is half the fun: life is much more manageable when thought of as a scavenger hunt as opposed to a surprise party."*

Like I said, I don't really have my own answers for some of this so I will share excerpts from my high school religion teacher's thoughts on death (whose faith and writing skills I have always admired):

Excerpts from "Death is Graduation"
by Lolita Jardeleza

"Over the years, I have come to the conclusion that perhaps the easiest way to understand death is to see it as our graduation to Eternity. When we finish 8th grade, we graduate and move on to high school. Then college, graduate school, and on to what you call "real life." When we graduate into eternity, we pass on to real "real life." Here are a few things to remember about death. No one escapes it. Everyone that was ever born dies eventually. We all have our turns. Psalm 139:16 says, "All the days ordained for me were written in Your book before one of them came to be." Do we expect our loved ones not to die? Do we get to call the shots as to when they die? If we answered "Yes" to these questions then we are dodging reality. Reality has proven time and again that we and our loved ones will all die. And we don't really have anything to say about when, where, who, why and how.

Those of us who believe in the teachings of Jesus know this much about what happens when we slip into eternity: "No eye has seen, no ear has heard, no mind has conceived what God has prepared for those who love Him." (1 Cor. 2:9) In other words not even our wildest imaginings can come close to the joys our Father has in store for our Homecoming. So death is not a fearsome thing. It is fearsome only when we focus on our separation from our dying loved one. Its desolate if we see God as a Cosmic Sadist who is bent on making us miserable instead of the loving Father who cannot do enough for us.

I look forward to that moment in my life when I step over the threshold of death and enter Eternity. And when I do, I shall sprint for Jesus and give Him a body hug which will take some doing because I won't have my body. We are also blessed in that we believe in the Resurrection; that death is not the end of all. We believe that someday we will all be reunited in our Father's house.

If you get to heaven before I do, please meet me at the Gate. If I get there before you do you can bet that I will be there at the Gate ready to give you my biggest hug. Jesus is the Resurrection and the Life and we who believe in Him will live even though we die. Though we will be separated, we will reunite. We will grieve but our grief will turn to joy. (John 16:17, 20)
"Death is turning out the lights because dawn has arrived."

I'm with Elvis - focus on life, and keep your mind and your options open.

~

One day I had a particularly difficult day at work. The job, the fifth or sixth that day, was about 45 minutes away. The wind was relentless. So much so that the heavy metal gate was being blown open and closed. Meanwhile the annoying crazy dog had to be kept in the yard. Repeatedly returning to my truck for parts for a frustrating repair I passed through the gate over and over with the wind and the dog making my life hell. It had been a long day and being tired and hungry caused my efficiency to drop. I would forget something and make an extra trip to the truck for myself. I was going crazy and felt like I couldn't take it anymore.

Finally, I finished the job and started the drive home. My light truck being buffeted by the wind the whole way and some precipitation starting to fall. Every so often a big gust would blast the truck sideways causing adrenaline rushes. The drive was not easy. As I made my way home I was unable to let go of my frustration and anger. I was all worked up and pissed.

Ahead on the road I see an ambulance. Traffic is slowing down. I soon see an absolutely mangled bicycle. Suddenly sobered from my anger, I realize that my day could have been worse. I felt almost guilty for being so upset with things I should be able to let go of. The feeling was similar to being called out on a mistake and having no response other than "I was wrong" "I'm sorry", or "I really messed up".

A good friend once told me "You don't want to leave this place unhappy." What if I had been struck down during my little temper tantrum?

So I think Death should instruct our lives. We ought to remember it and that it could happen from anything and at any time. I like this quote from the soundtrack to the move "*Ghost Dog, the Way of the Samurai*". The album has seven "Samurai code quotes" interspersed between songs, read by Forrest Whitaker who has a lead in the film:

"The way of the Samurai is found in death.
Meditation of inevitable death should be performed daily.
Everyday when one's body and mind are at peace,
They should meditate on being ripped apart by arrows, rifles, spears, and swords,
Being carried away by surging waves, Being thrown into the midst of a great fire,
Being struck by lightning, and shaken to death in a great earthquake,
Falling from thousand foot cliffs,
Dying of disease,
Committing seppiku at the death of one's master,
And everyday without fail, one should consider himself as dead.
This is the substance of the way of the Samurai."

So I think death is a metaphor for the immediacy of life. I also really like the quote from this month's prompt - "*Death is not the greatest loss in life. The greatest loss is what dies within us while we live.*"

To me this quote point to the same ideas as "don't leave this place unhappy". That every moment is precious. The death of a dream, a hope, a love, or one's spirit is so sad. Similarly, the death (or sacrifice) of hours of my time (the temper tantrum) is sad. Seeing the mangled bike instantly shifted my perspective.

I felt a feeling akin to embarrassment for holding on to negative feelings and not moving on. It truly felt like I had done something wrong by nurturing my frustrations. I take from this to live each moment well, keep death in mind, and live in a way that I am "ready" to leave.

~

Death is indeed inevitable. No matter how much we may wish to avoid it, death will ultimately reach each of us. For those who believe in the Supernatural, death is not necessarily the termination of life. Rather it is viewed as the separation of soul from the physical body and the continuation of life in another stage and form. Death, in religious context, then can be viewed as the gateway to hereafter. Much as the butterfly needs to progress through stages of its worldly existence, human beings also proceed through the stages of their lives...

The inevitability and unpredictability of worldly death increase the urgency on the wise to make the most of their lives. To the faithful it is a reminder that they cannot afford to focus their precious time with passing trivialities, at the cost of neglecting to prepare for the journey ahead of them.

"Every soul shall taste death, and only on the Day of Judgment will you be paid your full recompense." Quran

~

It is a really difficult topic. As a society, we really do not discuss this as a group. Maybe we should. It would be interesting to see what others believe and how they cope with it. I do envy the really religious folks who truly believe. Less worry!!! However, I think most human beings have a hope of something after. Not real belief, but hope. As I get older and see what the other folks in the scientific community believe, it gets harder. However, there does seem to be just the slightest bit of uncertainty. Remember, we are made of atoms just like the rest of the Universe. Maybe, after, we become a part of it. Quantum Mechanics makes anything possible. For me, to be able to retain my consciousness is the thing I really hope for. In the end, we will all see.

~

I think of death as a stopping point – like the end of a game. Just like a game, in which the purpose is generally to win, there is a purpose to our life and we are supposed to find out what that purpose is and devote our life to accomplishing that purpose. Death is that "pencils down" moment for our life.

I have no idea if there is anything after death, but I don't think that should have any impact result on how I live my life. I think to keep ourselves "on course", we should remind ourselves frequently that we have a finite amount of time to fulfill our purpose. A song that resonates with me is "Today" by John Hartford, which emphasizes the immediacy of the current moment:

"And every day I grow and die
As though it might be my last
And kiss the minute with a thankful smile
And turn my back on the past.",

So that's my view – death is a reminder to live a purposeful life. I'll offer one other quote that sums this up: "*Every man dies, not every man really lives*" (William Wallace)

ROUND 5: *WHAT DOES LOVE HAVE TO DO WITH IT?*

For Valentine's Day, I asked for thoughts on the topic of love. Here was my communication:

First off, here's a cool Gailic phrase that I came across on our current topic: "*A chuisle mo chroí*" – translated as the romantic endearment: "*pulse of my heart*".

The topic for round five was the challenging and extremely broad topic of love, with the following prompts provided:

- Romantic love
  - ○ Is this a trait of evolution to guarantee the "survival of the species"? Or something more meaningful?
  - ○ Is romantic love more about wanting something for yourself or wanting something for the other
- Familial love
  - ○ "*You don't choose your family. They are God's gift to you, as you are to them.*" (Desmond Tutu)
- Love for friends
  - ○ Here's a quote for you: "*I cut myself in the finger, and it pains me: this finger is a part of me. I see a friend hurt, and it hurts me, too: my friend and I are one*" (Nicola Tesla)

- Love for humanity
  - what keeps us from experiencing the love we have for our "loved ones" with humanity as a whole? Google "Dunbar's number" if you want to explore this a bit further

And a few additional quotes to get you thinking:

- *"Love is the answer, and you know that for sure; Love is a flower, you've got to let it grow"* (John Lennon)
- *"Where there is love, there is life"* (Gandhi)
- *"Let the beauty of what you love be what you do"* (Rumi)

~

As many contributors to WHWLSF had difficulty with the question of death, I for some reason don't seem to have much to say on the topic of love. There are tons of songs, poems, books, artworks, etc. which address love. I feel like what else can I add?

I suppose what I could offer up for consideration is Plato's ladder of love, from The Symposium. The idea of the ladder (here very crudely summarized) is that we are first drawn to the beauty of an individual and experience love. Then we realize that there are many beautiful bodies, and they are all similar beings. From there we see that the beauty of the soul/person outweighs the beauty of the body. (I'm sure many have experienced being with someone and they become more attractive as you come to see the beauty of their soul and character.) Next, we see beauty in activities, works, and institutions. We are inspired to make and do great things, and thus come to see the beauty of knowledge. At the highest rung of the ladder beauty is revealed in its pure form. We then contemplate the form of beauty itself.

Ascent of the ladder, according to this metaphor, is the evolution from the most basic physical love to a contemplation of the pure form of true beauty.

The stone carver Constantine Brancusi (known for his inscrutable finish work) would leave a small imperfection on each sculpture, symbolizing man's inability to attain the absolute. We have discussed how some things may be unknowable from our perspective, so maybe the ascent of the ladder is an ongoing process, like the quest for improvement in anything. The word Philosophy comes from ancient Greek. "Sophos" is wisdom, and "philos" is a kind of love that is forever seeking after. Those ancient Greeks had a word for every kind of love, "eros", "thumos", and the other ones I can't remember.

I know this entry smacks a bit of "I did my book report on. . .", but I really can't think of anything original to say about love. Perhaps this quote says it best, by (of course) Plato; "*Love is the name for our pursuit of wholeness, for our desire to be complete.*"

~

As usual, I have no "proof" that my thoughts/beliefs about love are true but as I live my life a conviction has grown and deepened that love is **everything**. It is the glue that holds the universe together. It is what constitutes everything that is. It is the benchmark to be used in making decisions, e.g., "what is the most loving choice?" Tennessee Williams writes in The Night of the Iguana that love is when one realizes that someone has burrowed his/her way into your heart. I like that realization because it touches on the mystery of why we love someone. Love isn't "achieved" by earning it. You don't have to be good in order to be loved. "*Look at the lilies of the field; they neither plow nor toil, yet Solomon in all his grandeur was not arrayed as one of these.*" At times however, (maybe most times) love is a decision rather than a feeling.

From a theological perspective, the idea of the Trinity - that God is three Persons but still One - says that God IS loving relationship. God **is** love. God is a verb more than a noun. And I am coming to believe that all of evolving creation is a form of God›s love giving birth.

Troubling questions about love concern a feeling of helplessness after becoming aware of the terrible suffering of so many in the world. Starving children, refugees, pain...the list goes on seemingly endlessly. I live with so many material comforts while most of the world lack sufficient resources. Not good, but I struggle with how to respond. Light a candle? Thoughts and prayers? Not enough. But am I called to sell all that I have and give it to the poor? My brother-in-law once said that, "money doth make cowards of us all." And what about Dunbar's number? I'm obviously still wrestling with this aspect of love.

I'll sign off with a poem by Meister Eckhart

Love Does That
"All day long little burro labors, sometimes
with heavy loads on her back and sometimes just with worries
about things that bother only burros.
And worries, as we know, can be more exhausting
than physical labor.
Once in a while a kind monk comes
to her stable and brings a pear, but more than that,
he looks into the burro's eyes and touches her ears
and for a few seconds the burro is free
and even seems to laugh,
because love does that.
Love frees."

Familial love - Familial love runs deep and probably never goes away entirely even when circumstances warrant its demise – incest, abuse, control or external influences. Children seem to always want to remain with their parents, no matter what, perhaps in the hopes that they will change and become better people and give them the love that they crave and see on TV and read in books. Or perhaps, it is just because children see their parents as necessary for survival. Children continue to seek their parents' approval no matter how many times it is withheld or worse, made to think they are losers. It seems that they need this approval in order to progress in their life. Without the vocal or demonstrated support of their parents' adult children are side tracked in their own happiness and progress in life because they continue to make decisions with the eye towards obtaining parental approval. How sad it is to grow up in such an environment. Our society does not seem to have the system in place to encourage and aid children and adults to cope with this situation in order to free them to live their own life.

Sibling love – I always wanted to grow up with a family like The Waltons on TV. It took me years to realize that this version of a family was rare and certainly not mine. Until I accepted this, I continually looked at other families assuming that they were the Waltons and wishing I could join them and forget mine. The baggage of sibling history comes and grows with you each year. I eventually realized that I would be happy in my own family by accepting the personality (good and irritating) of each person, but also, accepting that if that sibling continued to create angst that was not acceptable to me living a happy and healthy life I had my permission to completely cut out communication with them without feeling guilty. Yes, I wish it could be otherwise, but circumstances do not allow that to be and reality is that this person will always be loved as my sibling but cannot be included in my current life.

Friends – Love for friends can be just as strong as familial love, but it is developed over time and not instantly due to a biological connection. It is wonderful to be able to choose friends that you add to your own personal family to enrich your life via their support and joy of living.

Romance – Romantic love is too influenced by Movies, books, etc. If you are lucky enough to find a companion to walk through the happiness and hazards of life for even a moment in time, embrace the moment, do not dwell on whether it will last.

Love for Humanity – Given the ramifications of the last political election and aftermath, I am ashamed at the human capacity for hate and human degradation of others. I fear the capacity for love for humanity is being pushed aside and being unrewarded.

~

A Few Thoughts on Love

Thinking about love and expressing it is akin to thinking about God and then describing God. One can talk about it, but words limit the expansiveness of the state of love or being in love (and words surely limit God's nature). Instead, we hold up a figurative mirror and then are able to talk about what we see, feel, hear that sketch out what we believe to be love. (Since no one has seen God, we trust that Jesus is part of that triune God and shows humans what is God-like. Hence, Jesus serves in this picture as a mirror.)

I looked up how many book titles have the word love in them. In the Kindle Store alone, there are more than 56,000 of them. I didn't investigate the number of love poems or sonnets, movie titles, plays and so on. It must be that love is a very popular subject and everyone has a version to parse and share.

Fannie Flagg wrote a book *Standing in the Rainbow.* What a great title. I think that is how I experience love. When surrounded by love, romantic, familial, communal, you may not even be aware that you are in it, but you are very much aware of your euphoria. The sensation of love – "standing in the rainbow" – never grows old.

I think people use the word love as a catchall term. "I love mashed potatoes." Well, mashed potatoes do not love you in return. Mashed potatoes are, then, a favorite food and when you eat them, you really, really enjoy them. "I love Holst's *The Planets.*" Again, it does not love you in return. When you listen to this music it transports you in a pleasant way and stimulates your mind.

Human relationships are fragile. Even the closest ones are. It is love and trust that keeps friendships chugging along through the years, when people forget to call, or say the wrong thing, or do any number of things that are hurtful or cringe-worthy. Consider also that for most people there is memory of only three generations going back in time: You, your parents, and your grandparents. So, relationship in families' dissolves after a few short generations. Family bonds mean a lot, certainly. But then there are the dysfunctional families; is there love in them as well? That is likely, but it is not the nurturing love I think you selected for this topic.

To me, there is no truth in "one true love." I think there could be any number of people that a person could fall in love with. Humans are so very complicated, and during the course of a lifetime, different love interests can and do meet a person's needs for love and companionship. I am not advocating for changing partners, just that someone can love more than one person. No guilt required.

An old song from the 1960s has these words in the lyrics: "*I won't live in a world without love.*" Whenever things look bleak, it has helped me to pour on a little more love. It helps.

God is Love.

~

As always, I find the topic a little intimidating so I'll keep this short. Love is important because I think in general we are willing to dig deeper in defense of a loved one the we are for ourselves. In life we need more reasons to look beyond ourselves.

In the immortal words of Jimmy Buffett – *"I've always looked at life as a voyage, mostly wonderful, sometimes frightening. In my family and friends, I have discovered treasure more valuable than gold."*

I think this is a good quote because when you talk about discovered treasure you mean something that it took some sort of a journey to find. That is true for our loved ones. We are born with family but sometimes the things that are closest to us are the hardest to appreciate. Friends come in many different and unexpected ways. There is an art to identifying and appreciating friends and family. When you do, you understand what an important thing they are.

~

I think Love is the purpose and meaning of life. I think that to both receive <u>and</u> give love are basic human needs. Recently, a client of my husband's, died and left everything to the DC Humane Society. He was 96, had lived with his sister and his brother and taken care of them until they each died. Within a year of his brother dying, he died. No kids, no cousins, no nieces/nephews. I think taking care of and loving his siblings was what kept him alive. After that, loving animals gave meaning to his life.

Romantic love - In Greek "eros?" I think it is more meaningful than survival of the species. I think it is more about wanting something for the other person.

Familial love - In Greek "storge?" I think the most important and basic of these is parental love for children. I have read that children who don't experience parental love as an infant (or some sort of substitute) i.e. orphans, will never develop correctly psychologically or socially. Baby monkeys kept from their mothers offered the option of a metal source of milk vs. a soft, warm dummy (i.e. loving) will choose to starvation over lack of "love." Also important is sibling love. These are the people you will know and be supported by for the longest chunk of time in your life. They know and share your childhood experiences. One theory of why humans live so long is the Grandparent theory. Children who have loving Grandparents are more likely to survive than those who don't. So many geneticists feel that familial love is a main reason why our species has evolved to live as long as we do.

Love for friends - In Greek "philia?" Some friends are friends of convenience-i.e. coworkers or neighbors. You might or might not love but you are friendly with them to make your life/work better. Some people are friends because you have a fun time with them. But the best friends are those who support you, want the best for you and love you even though they know your flaws. You don't choose your family, but you do choose your friends (or they chose you.)

Love for humanity - I think Dunbar's number is more about how many people you can keep track of/get along with/ remember the names of, rather than how many people you can "love?" An example of love for humanity could be my son donating every single cent of the $19.75 he laboriously earned over the summer of 1st grade to tsunami victims. He didn't know them, he just saw they were suffering and cared. I remember saying to him, why don't you keep some of that money for yourself? and him saying he wanted them to get all of it. True love, from a small child, with no chance of him benefiting? That sort of proves that love is an extremely early, basic human emotion.

~

My daughter talked to me about the concept of "Eusociality", which is fascinating to me. (With some help from Wikopedia), Eusociality is described as the highest level of organization of animal sociality, which includes cooperative broodcare, care of overlapping generations within a colony of adults, and a division of labor into reproductive and non-reproductive groups. Some examples of Eusocial societies include ants, bees, wasps, termites, naked mole-rats and some shrimps. Scientists have debated whether humans are Eusocial, but the majority of evolutionary biologists believe that we are not Eusocial. Two thoughts on this: 1) it's interesting that, in some respects, termites, naked mole-rats, and some shrimp have more advanced systems for taking care of their older members and working together to take care of each other's children, and 2) doesn't debating about whether humans are eusocial seem much funner than the ridiculous amount of time we (and the vast majority of cable news) collectively spend debating our current political environment and more specifically forty-five? I want to start hanging out evolutionary biologists.

Anyway, back to the topic of love, another term for Eusocial social units is a "superorganism". I think that through evolution or some other mechanism, we are coming to the realization that all life (and non-life) is a superorganism. And that super organization may be the concept of God.

~

I once had to take a final exam in a Philosophy course which was conducted as a conversation in my Jesuit Professor's office. The time was 1973. The subject matter was a book by Rollo

May entitled: *Love and Will*. May was an American existential psychologist and author of the influential book Love and Will (1969). He is often associated with humanistic psychology, existentialist philosophy and, alongside Viktor Frankl, was a major proponent of existential psychotherapy.

In *Love and Will*, May said that the world has equated love with sex and will with power.

May felt that is was proper to pair love and will because both imply concern, positive acts and responsibility. Care is also a part of this equation with respect to love. As a verb, the dictionary defines care as "concern or interest; attach importance to something, or to look after and provide for the needs of."

May said that there are four kinds or forms of love in Western tradition.

Sex - He believed that Americans no longer view sex as a natural biological function but have become preoccupied with it to the point of trivialization. (Who can deny that the latter is extant in almost all of our culture and much of our advertising.)

Eros - is a psychological desire that seeks an enduring union with a loved one. It may include sex, but it is built on care and tenderness. it is the act of love, not the manipulation of organs.

Philia - an intimate nonsexual friendship between two people, takes time to develop, and does not depend on the actions of the other person.

Agape - is an altruistic or spiritual love that carries with it the risk of playing God. Agape is undeserved and unconditional.

In another observation, the first and second great commandments speak of the importance of love. Love is elevated above all else in those commandments.

Lastly, there is a building on my former college campus inscribed with a quote from Robert Southwell S.J.:

Robert Southwell (c. 1561 – 21 February 1595), also Saint Robert Southwell, was an English Roman Catholic priest of the Jesuit Order. He was also a poet, hymnodist, and clandestine missionary in post-Reformation England. The inscription/quote says "Not where I breathe, but where I love, I live."

~

Whatever "love" is, I think it is the only way we really see each other and the way we can transcend our individualism and recognize the godliness in ourselves and everyone else. But Lao Tzu, the Beatles, and Joseph Campbell articulate this better than me:

"Being deeply loved by someone gives you strength, while loving someone deeply gives you courage." (Lao Tzu)
"And in the end the love you make is equal to the love you take" (Beatles)
"What is the kingdom? It lies in our realization of the ubiquity of the divine presence in our neighbors, in our enemies, in all of us. " (Joseph Campbell – Thou Art That: Transforming Religious Metaphor"

~

LOVE: One's ultimate goal is to instill actionable awareness and empathy in overcoming one's ego and inaction towards doing good by sacrificing one's self interests or favor expectations for the benefit and welfare of others or nature. Baruch Spinoza best argues that the way to "blessedness" or "salvation" for each person involves an expansion of the mind towards an intuitive understanding of God, of the whole of nature and its laws so that life becomes a spiritual practice, whose goal is happiness and liberation. A free person is one conscious of the necessities that compel us all to discover to know what is good inside of you, such as love, and how to exemplify it in producing good outside of you through connectedness with family, friends, humanity and nature and to be thankful by giving of self toward others without personal gain of any kind.

~

A couple ideas of Plato come to mind when I think of the topic of love.

The first is from "Symposium" – and it is the idea that our souls are "separated before birth" and love it the attempt to reunite the soul. Here are two quotes from "Symposium":

"According to Greek mythology, humans were originally created with four arms, four legs and a head with two faces. Fearing their power, Zeus split them into two separate parts, condemning them to spend their lives in search of their other halves."
"Love is simply the name for the desire and pursuit of the whole."

The second concept by Plato that comes to mind is his "Allegory of the cave". Now this might be just a little of a stretch on the concept of love, but the allegory of the cave is that we (humanity) are a group of people who are chained to the wall of a cave. All we can see is shadows on a wall of the cave. Since this is all we can see, we believe this is the only reality. If we are freed, we will realize that the shadows on the wall were the result of things passing in from of the sun (or a fire). I think Plato thought that philosophy was the way to free ourselves to see true reality. I think, however, that the experience of "love" in whatever form we experience it – romantic, friendship, familial – that is the closest insight we can get to "true reality".

~

First off, let me say that I don't understand what love is. I have been in love and I have fallen out of love, but that does not explain what love actually is from a scientific view. I am not sure that love is unique to humans in that other animals choose one mate for life. It is also interesting how being in love can change perception and one's view of reality. In other words, people look past some bad elements of another person when they are in love with them, which is interesting. Is the person in love fooling themselves or does whatever love is actually change a person's perception of reality?

The concept of marrying for love is a relatively modern concept. Most couples in the past were together for convince or a part of an arranged marriage in the past, which is still the case in some cultures even now. The interesting part is that couples that were wed as part of an arranged marriage fell in love. To me, that is absolutely fascinating. Did they grow to love each other due to circumstances and close mutual existence, or was it something else? Another interesting phenomenon is couples that are in love that don't particularly like each other. Everyone has met couples that have been together for a long time that bicker and disagree about a lot of topics, but can't imagine life without their mate. Fascinating.

~

Maybe the desire for love is the skill that lets us search for the connection to the bigger entity and lets us either temporarily or permanently escape our ego-centric orientation. The act of love and the feeling of being in love provides us a partial sense of this connection – whether to a lover, your children, family, or friends. Even extending the word "love" to things like sports teams or other passions is relevant, I think. My brother is a big fan of going to his alma mater's college basketball games. Years ago, I asked him what he got from this – he said it was the feeling of connection with the others.

~

On the topic of love, I was struck by the following quote from the author and professor Brene Brown that we have a "*deeply held belief that we're inextricably connected to each other by something greater than us. And that thing that is greater than us is rooted in love and compassion — that there's something bigger than us and that we are connected to each other in a way that cannot be severed.*"

How can we love better? - One other quote by Brene Brown: "*Vulnerability is the birthplace of love*"

ROUND 6: *THE THREE "RS" – DO WE PARTICIPATE IN REBIRTH, REDEMPTION, AND RENEWAL?*

In the beginning of April 2018, and following the earth's cycles, we moved on to headier topics. Here was the prompt:

So, as we find ourselves in the season of spring, Easter, Passover, beginning of baseball season, NFL draft, and the run-up to the 2018 mid-term elections, I propose that we share thoughts on the topics of rebirth, redemption, and renewal *within* our lifetimes (as opposed to thoughts on after life considerations). As always, you have taken the topics in all different interesting directions and I encourage you to continue to do so. Here are a couple of prompts:

- *It is important never to lose faith in the possibility of profound inner change"* (Ian McEwan (Solar))
- What are some "conversion" stories (like St Paul's journey to Damascus) that resonate with you and what meaning do you get from them?

- Do you have a personal story to share where you or someone you know took a different, permanent, and positive new direction?
- What are some ways to promote "profound inner change"?
- *"Everyone thinks of changing the world, but no one thinks of changing himself."* (Leo Tolstoy) – is it possible to "change yourself and you will change the world?" If so, what does that mean in our current political and social environment?
- *"Emancipate yourselves from mental slavery. None but ourselves can free our minds"* (Bob Marley – Redemption Song) – How can we create a "inner revolution"?

The responses included really interesting observations and questions such as: the idea that renewal/rebirth is more about subtraction then addition, how does the creator view him/herself?, what is more meaningful – an idealized, childlike version of the truth, or a more adult, view where our heroes are more fallible people?, the idea that ideas inspire and are "reborn" in others, the idea that every day is about death and rebirth, and so many more interesting thoughts!

Read and enjoy for yourself....

⁓

Scientific studies have shown that changing the way we eat, exercise, meditate etc. can contribute to better health, but I wouldn't really call that transformation. I believe that transformation occurs but is rarely if ever accomplished by brute force or will power. Will power is an ego driven attempt to control and be the dominant driver. Rather, I think that transformation is more relational. Just as Everything is profoundly relational (even our bodies which couldn't function without the microbiome that have conjoined with us since birth). If one relinquishes into a willingness and wanting-ness to be transformed into one's truest and deepest self, the self that was "meant to be", the self that the world needs, then I believe that each of us has a true north orientation that will lead us into who we really are. But it is more subtraction than addition. More about letting go of fixed ideas about what we "should" think and feel and do, and trusting that holding loving desire is enough. If we can allow the loving desire to welcome the power of the universe/God/Higher Power into our selves, then we may freely "become" a new and transformed self, no longer I but now we. As St. Paul puts it, *"I have been crucified with Christ and I no longer live, but Christ lives in me."*

And the awesome, wonderful irony of it all is that the desire that leads us home is originally the desire of the One who "calls" us.

~

Here's a couple unconnected thoughts on this topic – all related to podcasts that I have listened to in the past few months.

The podcast *Match Made in Marrow* from Radiolab tells the story of a woman, Jennell Jenney, who is a bone marrow donor for Christian Evangelist magician/preacher, Jim Munroe. Jim incorporates the story of the bone marrow transplant as a spiritual rebirth in a Christian context and attributes his "rebirth" to Jennell. What's interesting is that Jennell Jenney is an atheist. Their different perspectives and discussions on the "meaning" of the bone marrow donation and Jim's recovery are interesting – he views it as a miracle and proof of God, she views it as a medical procedure. One of the ironies is that from Jim's religious perspective, his "savior", Jennell, will not go to heaven because she does not believe in God.

To me, this story raises an interesting question of possible different perspectives of the savior/creator versus the person who is saved/created. What if God has the perspective as Jennell – that creating the universe is not a miracle and that the creator/savior is not perfect, infallible, or omnipotent – maybe just a higher-level scientist/engineer who can create things and sacrifice (in Jennell's case, her bone marrow) to help his/her creation.

I'm not really doing the story justice – check it out for yourselves:

https://itunes.apple.com/us/podcast/radiolab/id152249110?mt=2&i=1000394633991

Also, if you are between the ages of 18-44 and want to volunteer to be bone marrow donor – here's how to do it: https://bethematch.org/support-the-cause/donate-bone-marrow/join-the-marrow-registry/

The second podcast that made me thing about your topic is *On Being with Krista Tippett* – in her discussion with angel Kyodo Williams, an ordained Zen priest and the author of *Being Black: Zen and the Art of Living with Fearlessness and Grace*. In their discussion, Krista Tippett makes the comment that: "*We have not trained ourselves to do that work that is upon us*"

That quote resonates with me – I believe that we are all called to do something important, but that most of us, and definitely me, are not preparing ourselves for the "work that is upon us".

~

For whatever reason, this topic has me thinking about the author Harper Lee and her books *To Kill a Mockingbird* and *Go Set a Watchman*. *To Kill a Mockingbird* is my favorite book all time. The character Atticus Finch is one of the greatest character heroes ever written.

Initially I was drawn to *To Kill a Mockingbird* for this topic because a central theme of the book is that you come to understand people by walking a mile in their shoes.

"You never really understand a person until you consider things from his point of view... Until you climb inside of his skin and walk around in it".

In terms of inner change, inner revolution, I think that the way to do it is not from introspectively looking inside yourself. I think inner change comes from looking at the world from the perspectives of others.

The author Harper Lee was an interesting character. She was not a very public person, and despite many rumors about her working on other books, those close to her say she was sworn to never write another book. Shortly before she died, a second book was published that she wrote called "Go Set a Watchman". It is controversial because it was published in her old age, and many think that she wasn't capable of giving her permission to publish the book. Also, there is controversy as to whether the book was written as a sequel to *To Kill a Mocking-bird* or as its first draft.

I was conflicted about reading the book given the circumstances under which it was published but ultimately read *Go Set a Watchman*. It is set twenty years after *To Kill a Mocking-bird* when Scout is an adult. It also features Atticus but provided a very different picture. Almost the opposite picture. In *To Kill a Mockingbird*, Scout reveres her father who is a flawless character. In *Go Set a Watchman*, as an adult, Scout learns that her father is affiliated with some anti-segregation groups and she is she terribly disillusioned. As a reader who also considers Atticus to be a hero, I was disillusioned too.

I've given this story a lot of thought since reading it. I decided that Atticus still gets to be a hero. In *To Kill a Mockingbird* we believe that Atticus made the choices he made because they supported his deep seeded beliefs in equality. In *Go Set a Watchman,* we learn that Atticus wasn't an equal rights advocate, but stood on the side of legal justice. In a way, to me, Atticus is more heroic as a more human flawed character who does the right thing. The most noteworthy thing to me about second picture of Atticus is the fact that in the end he didn't pollute his children with the racism that he struggled with. In the end, Scout reaches a new level of maturity when she comes to understand that she needs to live her life guided by her own morals not just mimicking the morals that she felt she understood from her father. That is its own inner revolution.

It is unclear how much of the books are based on Harper Lee's real-life experiences. Her father was a small-town lawyer, and the legal case in *To Kill a Mockingbird* is similar to a case her father was involved with. Fact or fiction, Harper Lee's book has been read by millions of readers young and old and has definitely changed the world for the better.

Anecdotal side note on the Tolstoy quote – I'm guessing I'm the only member of the group with a painting of Tolstoy hanging in my house.

Hope this answers the question!

~

I recently came across a very cool word that emphasizes that rebirth/redemption are the result of a process: The term is: <u>liminality</u>, which is defined as the *"quality of ambiguity or disorientation that occurs in the middle stage of rites, when participants no longer hold their pre-ritual status but have not yet begun the transition to the status they will hold when the rite is complete."* In this context, I think this means that if you desire rebirth/redemption, you need to follow a process, be open to a changed perspective, and be prepared for "dark nights" of confusion that are required before rebirth.

~

Responding to your prompts:

"It is important never to lose faith in the possibility of profound inner change" **(Ian McEwan (Solar))"**

Solar Energy would be a profound change for a planet that many fear is perhaps past the point of fixing due to climate change. The building of a Solar energy facility is implemented by Professor Beard who feels he is too old to accomplish anything more of value. Then goes on to have both a kid (albeit unwanted) and a professional resurgence (albeit with an idea stolen from a guy he murdered) a decade later. But, whatever his motives and however it happened, if Professor Beard had been successful at implementing large scale solar energy, it would possibly have a huge, positive impact on the world.

What are some "conversion" stories (like St Paul's journey to Damascus) that resonate with you and what meaning do you get from them?

I always like the CS Lewis story of the very reluctant convert: *"You must picture me alone in that room at Magdalen, night after night, feeling, whenever my mind lifted even for a second from my work, the steady, unrelenting approach of Him whom I so earnestly desired <u>not</u> to meet. That which I greatly feared had at last come upon me. In the Trinity Term of 1929 I gave* in, and admitted that God was God, and knelt and prayed: perhaps, that night, the most dejected and reluctant convert in all." I also like St. Francis of Assisi's conversion (at least I really like the Franco Zeffirelli Brother Sun, Sister Moon movie version of his conversion). Also, St. Augustine "*Lord make me pure, but not yet!*"

Do you have a personal story to share where you or someone you know took a different, permanent, and positive new direction?

Having kids of course. That totally changes your life and your goals in a hugely positive, permanent direction. Also, I recently started yoga. It is a small, but arguably positive change. Does that count?

What are some ways to promote "profound inner change"?

I think it often begins with a "quest". I think it often arises from a deep distaste for the current situation. Or an attempt to fix one small corner of the world.

"Everyone thinks of changing the world, but no one thinks of changing himself." (Leo Tolstoy) – is it possible to "change yourself and you will change the world?" If so, what does that mean in our current political and social environment?

I like that you picked a quote from Tolstoy - the writer my Grandfather did his PhD thesis on. I've read a couple books about him. Tolstoy had a "conversion experience" from member of the nobility/soldier to a non-violent pacifist/anarchist/supporter of serfs. He started schools for serfs. I've read that his school at Yasnaya Polyana was really the start of the Democratic Education movement. And Tolstoy's <u>A Letter to a Hindoo</u>

(or Hindu) may have inspired Gandhi: *'Do not resist evil, but also do not yourselves participate in evil–in the violent deeds of the administration of the law courts, the collection of taxes and, what is more important, of the soldiers, and no one in the world will enslave you"* (Tolstoy's letter). *"Tolstoy's life has been devoted to replacing the method of violence for removing tyranny or securing reform by the method of non-resistance to evil. He would meet hatred expressed in violence by love expressed in self-suffering."* (Gandhi's interpretation/comment on Tolstoy's letter). And then Gandhi inspired Martin Luther King and that helped the civil rights movement.

Of course, if one person changes themselves, it usually doesn't accomplish a whole lot. But, I do think one person's change inspires another person's change. That can be for the good or the bad. If one person shows up on the shift with a really bad attitude, it can throw the entire, perfectly previously happy group into a bad state. Conversely, one person with an unshakeable positive attitude can flip a group with a bad attitude. In our current environment, I think it is REALLY important for everyone else to act decent or else one person's indecency can spread to the rest of the country. I am reading Comey's book: *A Higher Loyalty*. And whatever else you think of him, he seems like a really decent guy who managed to remain decent in a bad situation.

"*Emancipate yourselves from mental slavery. None but ourselves can free our minds*" (Bob Marley – Redemption Song) – How can we create a "inner revolution"?

I read that this song was written after Bob Marley was diagnosed with melanoma (that killed him at only age 36?!? - I did not realize he died that young). I think often when you realize abruptly that life is short, that is a huge trigger for inner change. I also read that Marley was quoting Marcus Garvey *"We are going to emancipate ourselves from mental slavery because whilst others might free the body, none but ourselves can free the mind."* His life was kind of sad-founder of Pan-Africanism, imprisoned for fraud while trying to implement a plan (arguably both racist and harmful for African Americans) to start a shipping company to repatriate African-Americans back to Africa. (sort of like Professor Beard in Solar, yes, he committed fraud but it was in the course of trying to accomplish something he felt was hugely good). Although Marcus Garvey did not succeed in his quest, he inspired Marley and then Marley inspired Robert Shriver and Bono to start Product Red and One Campaign which (incredibly?) funds ¼ of the work to fight AIDS, ½ of the work to fight TB and ¾ of the work to fight malaria in Africa. Which is Huge.

Overall, most people are not going to create or develop something huge within their lifetime. And most people don't get reborn, redeemed or renewed in a huge way. But if they renew something small, maybe they can accomplish little good things that together can accomplish a lot of good. And someone who is on the receiving end of the little bit of good may one day be inspired, partly because of that little good to do or write or create something that turns out to be Really Good. Comey cites his boss at his teenage grocery store stocker job as his inspiration, Tupac (*"Don't leave this world without giving it your all"*) cites a high school English teacher, Lincoln credited his stepmother, Dorothy Height cites a neighbor who advocated for the town Elks to pay for college, Biggie cites a middle school English teacher, Dorothea Dix cites a kind grandmother who rescued her from alcoholic parents, Eisenhower cites a coach, Mary Church Terrell cites a nurse, Thyra Edwards cites a hairdresser, J.K. Rowling may have been inspired by her school's principal, Steve Jobs cites a 4th grade teacher.

So, a "small" kindness from a "regular" person like middle school teacher can have a big impact later (or get a Wizard Headmaster modelled after you. (*"we must all face the choice between what is right and what is easy" "Words are, in my not-so-humble opinion, our most inexhaustible source of magic. Capable of both inflicting injury, and remedying it." "Happiness can be found even in the darkest of times, if one only remembers to turn on the light.*"-Dumbledore is a good source of quotes)

~

I'm reading "Gilead" by Marilynne Robinson and came across this:

"He may, so to speak, have been too dazzled by the great light of his experience to realize that an impressive sun shines on us all... Sometimes the visionary aspect of any particular day come to you in the memory of it, or it opens to you over time....I believe there are visions that come to us only in memory, in retrospect."

I really like that – the idea that figuring things out is not a singular event – it is in the "rebirth" of an experience or experiences into meaning/purpose over time and through the reinterpretation of our system of memory. Maybe we should be more purposeful about how we evaluate and interpret our everyday experiences.

~

I immediately thought of sleeping. Every day we and the other animals have some sort of sleep cycle. Sleeping and waking to a new day is kind of miraculous. If we sleep deep enough, there is a bewilderment when we awaken. For myself, for a nanosecond, I have no identity in this moment. I am like a newborn unaware of what the world holds for it. (The end of the day can thus be likened to a death, and the morning a rebirth.) Of course, then I remember my schedule and I am back to being the same person as yesterday. Then I drink coffee, which is, quite literally, a godsend. The midwife of my morning.

Death and rebirth is happening everywhere, all the time, and all around us. I think of plants and their cycles: Seed, germination, grow to a plant or tree, make flowers and perhaps fruits, then more seeds and continue. Some are annual, and others have longer cycles. Some insects live for only days. If I step back, I see that we are just another creature with its particular cycle. It seems to me completely natural like the seasons.

I don't mean to upset anyone, but while thinking about this topic I thought of this. Birth and re-death. I was thinking of fruit blossoms that get killed in late frosts. Then I thought of Abraham Lincoln's son, children and babies, the dead tree that nobody watered, and the huge percentage of hatchling sea turtles that don't survive. I guess I'm trying to point to some inverse to rebirth, like when one has their greatest hopes or expectations dashed. Electricity has a forward current and also a reverse current in a circuit. These re-deaths seem to me natural too. However, I don't feel I have reached any conclusions nor do I have any great insight into this.

In my opinion, this month's topic, and really all of them, tie into the very first one. Whatever OUR perception of love, death, life, etc., we are somehow able to fathom the idea that OUR perception is not the only, and that it has limitations. (Though the question of whether things so metaphysical can ever be completely known is open for debate, perhaps eternally.) Dogs see so much with their noses, bats with sonar, and blind wind scorpions with their pedipalps. Knowing there are myriad perceptions of the same thing still leads me back to the beginning question. What are we, what is this, and why??

I also thought of the dinosaurs, and scales of death and rebirth. From insects to global events. I will pose this question: What will the next death and rebirth of the world look like? At the rate that things are going, and the unpredictability of it all, the world feels like it is reaching some kind of critical mass. Even the sun has a lifespan! If all or most people go the way of the dinosaurs, what will happen? Might unforeseen uses of technology, and unforeseen cooperation amongst people and nations save Earth? Will we find an alien real-estate planet broker in another solar system? Will our new planet be a "fixer-upper" or really new? Just some thoughts, and so I ask; What does the next big rebirth/change look like to you when you try to imagine it?

~

I think I may have seen a reference to the good thief earlier in this project and maybe that triggered my thought on the topic of redemption/rebirth. After a life of crime, punishment, and soon to be death, he recognizes who he is next to, he says: *"we have been condemned justly, for the sentence we received corresponds to our crimes, but this man has done nothing criminal."* Then he said, *"Jesus, remember me when you come into your kingdom."* [43] He replied to him, «Amen I say to you, today you will be with me in Paradise." Luke 23:39–43.

'*Today you will be with me in Paradise*" is to me one of the most beautiful, comforting, and mysterious phrases I have encountered. In terms of rebirth and redemption, I think it means that we just need to realize the simple truth that we are all one organism – there's no such thing as you versus me, us versus them, me versus it - *"Love one another as I have loved you"*

Did the good thief get lucky to have the opportunity to find himself next to Jesus and have the opportunity to ask and receive salvation? I don't think so – I think the point of the story is that we all have the same opportunity to come to this realization.

When I thought of this, I researched this story. I was surprised to find that in the Gospels of Matthew and Mark, both of the men crucified next to Jesus rebuked him.

What does this mean? First off, the Luke gospel story is so beautiful and powerful, that I'm going to go with that version over Matthew and Mark. To me, I believe that knowledge/wisdom are available to us if we seek it out. We will see "Jesus" in those around us. But in another way, I believe that the "good" was going to be in paradise that day whether he praised Jesus or rebuked him. What type of god would need his children, created in his image and likeness, to worship him? If got created us as his children, he would love them unconditionally. I don't see any other way.

Would I have recognized Jesus if I was dying on a cross next to him? I have to admit I think that I probably wouldn't. I think I would be distracted by the pain and if I wasn't on a cross, I would probably be distracted by something else – probably with my head down looking at my phone.

~

It is an interesting thought. Usually, we think in society, of the reverse. Someone who was tranquil and normal, and because of some event, changes for the worse.

Actually, the stories of those who had a conversion based on an experience, and ended up a better person, are uplifting thoughts. These stories should be promoted.

I think society focuses too much on negative stories. That is where the ratings are. But, we should promote those many stories that promote positive change from within that helps those throughout.

A person can truly change for the better. If they can find those things and thoughts internally and/or externally, then society as a whole would benefit.

We should always try to find ways to improve ourselves. Think outwardly as opposed to inwardly.

~

When I was a kid, I read Thomas Merton's book: *The Seven Storey Mountain* and it make a strong impact on me as a conversion story. I wonder if I reread it today if it would I would make the same impression or if would be disappointing from my more jaded, adult perspective (like my second readings of *On the Road, Catcher in the Rye*, and *Travels with Charlie*).

But more interesting to me now is Thomas Merton's life after his "lightning bolt" conversion experience. He fought for years with his Abbot, many times threatening to leave the Abbey, and using his fame as leverage in his battles with the Abbot. He also had a love affair with a student nurse, "M", who was half his age that cared for him after neck surgery. This affair caused him to have to choose between his monastic life or a life with "M". He ultimately chose to renew his vow of obedience and chastity. In a sense this choice was a second conversion experience for him – the first one, the "lightning bolt" conversion is more appealing and sold many books. The second one is in some ways more authentic – made in anguish, shame, and at a very high price (true love). Did he make the right choice? Not to me – I'm pretty sure I would have picked "M" but the point to me is that redemption stories, especially "lightning bolt" experiences are imperfect and after the lightning bolt, we as humans, are still stuck with the same weaknesses we had before – insecurity, jealousy, pettiness, desire, etc. Our lives are works in process – for most of us, there's no moment of enlightenment, just moments of insight every now and then.

~

The Newsletter *Religion and Politics* (a project of the John C. Danforth Center on Religion and Politics of Washington University in St. Louis) once called Rheinhold Niebhur Washington's favorite Theologian. Niebhur has been quoted and referenced by Presidents Obama, Carter and Senator John McCain.

President Obama said there is *"serious evil in the world, and hardship and pain,"* and *"we should be humble and modest in our belief we can eliminate those things. But we shouldn't use that as an excuse for cynicism and inaction."*

President Jimmy Carter said, *"Niebuhr was always present in my mind in a very practical way, particularly when I became President and was facing the constant threat of a nuclear war, which would have destroyed the world."* In his 2007 book, John McCain dedicated a chapter to Niebuhr.

In an April 25, 2017 article in the aforementioned newsletter, the author states that *"Sin, irony, tragedy. These words leapt out of the pages of Niebuhr's books and speeches."* Humanity was fallen and redeemed through God's grace, Niebuhr wrote. But that *"redemption is always incomplete and we can never rise to the standards set forth in the Bible. Only by accepting our limitations could we make the best out of an imperfect situation. In a world full of evil, we must choose good, but we must accept that we can never get rid of sin entirely. The irony of our situation is that we must often do what is considered evil for the sake of good."*

Finally, one of the quotes from Niebuhr that stands out and loosely addresses our topic of redemption is:

"Nothing worth doing is completed in our lifetime; therefore we must be saved by hope. Nothing true or beautiful or good makes

complete sense in any immediate context of history; therefore, we must be saved by faith. Nothing we do, however virtuous, can be accomplished alone; therefore, we are saved by love. No virtuous act is quite as virtuous from the standpoint of our friend or foe as from our standpoint. Therefore, we must be saved by the final form of love which is forgiveness."

~

Counterintuitively, I think the dawning of the "Trump era" provides us individually and collectively, with a significant opportunity for renewal. First off, I didn't vote for the guy and have reoccurring feelings that his election must have been foretold in the book of Apocalypse as one of the signs of the end of times.

But, whether or not that's true, and maybe particularly if it is true, I think current events should challenge us (and me) to re-assess our believes, values, and actions, particularly how we have reacted to it.

In my view, Trump's election was in large part due to a triumph of the "forces of fear". When I hear people attributing Trump's election to that fact that people are "idiots" or "racists", I think they are missing something much more important, are missing an opportunity for personal growth, and are not taking responsibility for the underlying problems and fears that Trump so effectively exploited – institutionalized inequities build into our economic system and a social safety net that contributes to intergenerational poverty and hopelessness – all enabled by a very corrupt political system.

What is the opportunity? If you see politics or people in terms of "good vs evil", "my viewpoint vs idiots", or "my viewpoint vs racists" – challenge yourself to rethink your views. It's not that simple and that viewpoint will prevent us from ever having a discussion that can lead to a better world – immigration reform, welfare reform, drug addiction, education, economic inequity, etc. A simplistic viewpoint also makes you more like the people you think are narrow-minded "idiots". A recent article in the New York Times estimates that 9% of people who voted for Obama voted for Trump and that among white voters who had never been to college, it was 22%. Are these people racists? I don't think so – I think they made their choice based on a variety of factors; mostly, I believe, because they thought that Trump would improve their economic prospects and also out of a sense of anger at a political system that they believe has favored some over others. If we want a better world, we should focus on these people – understand their legitimate concerns, develop ideas that address their concerns and work to develop a broader coalition than trying to stitch together 51% voter edge over the other party.

~

I believe in constant evaluation and re-evaluation of my personal being and circumstances. I feel the need to think about my opinions about myself, my observations, politics, etc. to make sure that they still make sense. Some opinions change over time or change due to new information. That process is a type of regrowth. I find it disturbing that in our current political environment, that politicians cannot ever update an opinion due to personal growth or new scientific discoveries because it is viewed as weak or wishy-washy.

~

Rebirth, redemption, renewal and perhaps reincarnation all relate to my soul search and spirit; intangibles yet integral to my beliefs and faith to guide me on life's journey. To address them and confront my own doubts and conflicts in this material tangible world I confide in a time of quiet solitude each day to open my meditative thoughts to ask for any counsel the Holy Spirit may choose to grace me with. And in times of greater need I rely on the Rosary to help reconcile my physical self and ego through a good dosing of humble and pious reflection to get right with the Father. After all, in believing that the spirit with continue incorruptible as God's will and energy I must endeavor to prepare it for redemption from the body's corruptibility for renewal and rebirth.

ROUND 7: *WHY DO BAD THINGS HAPPEN?*

In early May 2018, after reading everyone's thoughts on re-birth, redemption, and renewal, and after talking with several participants on the project, I felt a sense of urgency to turn this project from an interesting thought exercise to an actual "result". Here are the questions I posed:

In our six rounds so far, we have thought about whether there is a purpose to our lives, how you find purpose, sources of in-sight, death, love, and rebirth. So... what comes next?

"To achieve great things, two things are needed: a plan and not quite enough time." (Leonard Bernstein)

With that in mind and to keep ourselves focused on achieving something important with a deadline in sight, and to complete this project in one year: round seven is a two part question:

> **Q1:** *Why is there so much pain, suffering, inequality in this world? Please include your thoughts on evil versus "acts of God": i.e., is there a difference between death caused by a murderous, evil dictator versus death by a meteor or other natural event?*

A couple of quotes to get you thinking:

- *"If time is not real, then the dividing line between this world and eternity, between suffering and bliss, between good and evil, is also an illusion."* (Herman Hesse)
- *"Mankind is not likely to salvage civilization unless he can evolve a system of good and evil which is independent of heaven and hell." (George Orwell)*
- *"It is not true that good can only follow from good and evil only from evil, but that often the opposite is true."* (Max Weber)

Q2: (Note this question was inspired by one of the submissions and our follow-up discussion) Paleontologists believe there have been five mass extinctions in the world to date. As a thought exercise, let's imagine that the earth may have supported intelligent life that went extinct and left no fossil record (not a completely unrealistic notion, by the way - see this recent Washington Post article: *"Could intelligent life have existed on Earth millions of years before humans?"*)

https://www.washingtonpost.com/national/health-science/could-intelligent-life-have-existed-on-earth-millions-of-years-before-humans/2018/04/20/9b13e7ac-433a-11e8-8569-26fda6b404c7_story.html?noredirect=on&utm_term=.db-61c965eb41

So, here's the question - assuming humans don't survive the 6th extinction, what might the next version of intelligent life be like? Or more specifically as per our colleague's question (slightly reworded): *What does the next incarnation of conscious life look like to you when you try to imagine it?*

So... in the words of Isabel Allende, let's TOGETHER *"Write what should not be forgotten."*

~

Responses to question 1:
This is a really difficult question because there is no really good answer. When we were kids, some of the Nuns seemed to imply that more suffering on earth meant less suffering in "Purgatory."

That did make sense to me at the time. But I began to question this when I saw suffering infants. They had no reason to go to "Purgatory?" So....you now come up with why suffering and "Why do bad things happen to good people?"

I have a much easier time coming to terms with suffering caused by natural events-it seems like physics caused it and it seems more understandable on some level. Less senseless on some level??? A hurricane results from warm water and low pressure and the same laws of physics that give us rain, sometimes give us hurricanes. There is a mathematical formula for hurricanes based on ocean temperature, *air pressure*, moisture, wind speed and *water* levels.

Human created misery is harder and seems less natural. I do think that "little, mean, almost thoughtless stuff" can escalate into "horrendous mean stuff." They say both Hitler and Stalin were abused as children. They were abused because something had happened to their parents etc. Combine that with some mental illness and perfect storm of social conditions and you have genocide. I remember when we were *"shock and awe-ing"* Iraq in the 2nd Gulf War. I was thinking of little kids in basements terrified of the bombs. And I thought "those kids will hate Americans forever." And I now wonder if that was the genesis of ISIS/ISIL? But that would be the opposite of your Max Weber quote?

And I do agree with him that sometimes adversity/evil triggers good instead of perpetuating evil.

I also think that the greed that results in severe inequality can, in the right circumstances, lead to such social resentment that it can lead to murderous revolutions. As we watch the Wall Street rich get richer (many of whom created the economic crisis) while honest, hard-working laborers, teachers and social workers get poorer and poorer, your question on inequality naturally arises. So, I think that means maybe we should all listen to Bernie!!!

~

Why is there so much pain, suffering, inequality in this world? Such an important question! I have often struggled with this subject and am still woefully in the dark in my efforts to understand. A few thoughts have risen to the surface but they remain relatively inchoate and unconnected. So, the work in progress for now....

Which is worse... a child accidentally drops a whole carton of eggs on the floor and they all break, making a big mess.... or a child angrily throws an egg on the floor, making a small mess? This touches slightly on the "acts of God" aspect. I think it's obvious that the question of the size of the mess is less relevant than the intention. (Although it's also relevant that the one child is angry and hasn't learned yet how to manage his/her feelings and needs help with this.) I do think that intentionally wanting to harm a person or any creature is "worse" than someone being afflicted with suffering through disease, natural disaster, etc. The malevolence involved in the intentional harm adds an element that hurts all creation; it "undoes" beauty and truth and goodness; it is a crime against the whole.

Creation is not complete, as evidenced by the existence of pain and suffering. In some deep and mysterious way, I believe each of us is called in a particular way to alleviate what we see wrong in the world, including both physical pain and social injustice. Why does a loving God allow terrible things to happen? I surely don't know, but possibly God "needs" us to co-create, that it is on us to work toward making the world what it needs to be.

Max Weber's quote suggests that every good act has a dark side and every bad act may yield a silver lining. I do believe this is true. Thinking in binary terms (good vs bad, true vs false, etc.) won't get us very far and will prevent creative problem-solving.

~

I don't think there is really an answer to why there are so many bad things in life. I think the real question is "There is so much pain, suffering, inequality in this world. What are you going to do about it?" I really liked the Niebuhr quote from the last set of answers that was: *"Nothing worth doing is completed in our lifetime; therefore we must be saved by hope."*

In a hard world with so many problems and so much need it is easy to feel like you can't fix it all so why bother. When traveling to Haiti one of the things that stays with me is the fact that there is never enough. When you serve 500 plates of food, the 501st and 600th child will go without because there is never enough. Walking away from a child that is hungry because there is no more food to give away is sobering thing. And you could let that reality convince you to stop trying. I think that real evil in the world comes from giving in to the hopelessness. I don't know why there is suffering and inequality, but I do know that there are many opportunities to do good in the world. Being hopeful, giving people hope and dignity is how you make it a little better.

I do think there is a difference between the badness that comes from a murderous dictator and that of a natural disaster. The damage is self-inflicted when it is perpetrated by a murderous dictator. Having read too many books about the terrible things of WWII – what always shocks me is how so many regular people allowed themselves to be dragged so deeply into the cruelty. That is the difference between a natural disaster and the terrible dictators – the dictators make many other people their accomplices thus exposing the very worst in us.

Dr. Paul Farmer spent a lot of time in Haiti predominantly focusing on trying to deal with drug resistant tuberculosis. His story is told in a book called: *Mountains Beyond Mountains*. The title of the book is taken from a Haitian proverb that is along the lines of *"Beyond mountains, there are mountains."* Basically, reaching the top of one mountain shows you the existence of the next mountain and the next beyond it. We won't ever right every inequality. We can't feed every kid. We can't escape the possibility that the next murderous dictator is planning the way to recruit willing accomplices in cruelty. We can try to help people. We can resolve not to ever be dragged down into the cruelty and we can share hope wherever possible.

In the immortal words of Jimmy Buffett:

"If a hurricane doesn't leave you dead it will make you strong. Don't try to explain it. Just nod your head. Breathe In, Breathe Out, Move On."

~

One act is a complete form randomness. Natural disasters or Acts of God and are random and very hard to predict. Over the centuries, as science evolved, the number of humans who have perished have gone down. We still have them and will always have them. Hopefully, in the future, as science becomes more important to mankind, the numbers will go down further.

For suffering, many humans die and suffer from disease. (Heart attacks, stroke, etc.). Again, science can lower these numbers. If sufficient funding was given to science, the numbers would go down further.

The rest are manmade and are direct cause of power. I think the sense of "power" corrupted humankind at all levels. Either thru power to dominate others, the use of religion as a weapon, the allure of having power over others is the main reason humankind has not gone further scientifically.

If, as a society, we used science as the tool to further mankind, as opposed to dominating others which historically we have done, there would be less suffering.

In seeing the countless ways over the centuries over millions of years, how many things had to happen for intelligent life to evolve, I see it more likely than not, we are the only intelligent life in the Universe. With the Earth tilted just enough off center to having a magnetic field to protect us from harmful radiation to the formation of the Moon in the early part of the formation of our solar system; to the asteroid impact that wiped out the dinosaurs that allowed the mammals to evolve....so many twists and turns. There are countless others.

Maybe, if humanity viewed our little blue planet as 1 place for intelligent life, then maybe we would treat it better and others as well. Otherwise, possibly, the only place in the Universe where intelligent life resides, will be wiped out by our own hand.

Third, and this actually gets to the question, I think of history as something like a relay race – consciousness arising at some point and handing some kind of "baton". I would argue the we humans are part of the chain starting with single-cell organisms propelling themselves toward heat, to prokaryotes, to water-based reptiles, to brave land-based reptiles (or more likely, water-based reptiles that were trying to escape bigger, stronger water-based reptiles), to tiny mammals, to primates, to us.

Now, if all our antecedents could talk, or more importantly write things down, I'm sure they all made amazing progress, but since we can think about this stuff and write it down, I would say that we took that baton and took this journey to another level – beyond the earth, beyond just scraping by, beyond just procreating as a way of "staying alive" after our deaths.

If humans become extinct, that doesn't bother me. If we're lucky, we are a really small part of an eons-long relay race with some type of purpose/destination. I have this image of the race as one where the last baton holder runs/escapes right out of the arena – transforming a competition of the pointless running around a circle to "beat" another runner to leaving the circle and the arena into the next level of consciousness – an understanding of why we are running around in circles competing against each other for no apparent purpose. And heading for the destination we have been preparing for thousands of generations....

～

Why is there so much pain, suffering, inequality in this world? One view that I have always held is that good and evil in this world are the result of our "free will". Misuse of free will can lead to moral evil and that can lead to physical evil. Many Christian apologists have said that free will exists so that love can exist. If free will did not exist we would not be capable of freely choosing love. What would occur in its place is a kind of programmed mechanical love. Ira Levin wrote a book, *The Stepford Wives*, which demonstrates the kind of soulless empty love of a robot as personified in the Stepford Wives.

To the point, God has allowed us to freely choose to love or not to love, both choices have consequences and their own results. Finally, take the case of the "evil" of natural disasters. Of course, floods, earthquakes and volcanic disruptions take their toll on human life and property. However, in an of themselves they are morally neutral. A single example of this might be the cataclysmic events that led to the destruction of the dinosaurs. The demise of dinosaurs led to the rise of mammals and the human race.

The Catechism says that God created the world in a state of journeying toward its ultimate perfection. In this evolution good and bad appear side by side, the perfect exist alongside of the imperfect.

~

There is so much suffering in the world because the universe is indifferent to our existence. We are a small planet in a small arm of a small galaxy in a very large universe. We have tried to find some universal or overreaching meaning to our existence, in part, to pad our own egos that we are the pinnacle of creation. The truth is that we are no different than any other living creature, on this planet or others. Suffering, tragedy, unfairness, inequality are all conditions that we judge for our existence and are quite subjective. While tragedies happen, I think they happen at the same rate or, more likely, less than previous generations. I think our access to media instantaneous around the world has made it seem that they are happening at a great pace than before, but most likely not. Our ancestors would never have heard about things happening across the globe from them, while we hear about it as is happening. As to the death of a victim, a perpetrator, a martyr, or a bystander; they are all the same in the end. The dead person is just that, dead. Justice and tragedy are concepts we made up to deal with those deaths.

Good vs evil is also very subjective in many cases. I think in terms of warfare, the judgement depends highly on the side that was victorious. The concept of evil has always been perplexing for me because there usually seems to be an attempt to explain away evil acts as being connected to a separate source or being, i.e., "He was possessed by the devil" or "they didn't worship the right god in the right way". Do I think that there are heinous and very bad acts; yes, but I think they are usually isolated to that act. I do not think there are extraordinary beings or forces that are at play for good or bad. Do I think that perpetrators of heinous or bad acts should be punished; yes by using the laws that we, as a society, made.

~

On Question 1, I understand this question on human condition from a religious perspective. If one believes that this existence is designed as a test for a future life, then it becomes necessary that opposites (i.e. good and evil, joy and suffering, plenty and misery, etc.) should be used to test people with. Through such tests, whether acts of God or men, both those affected (whether they show patience, faith, gratefulness, generosity, etc.) and those not directly affected (whether they rush to help the suffering, stand for justice, exhibit jealousy or disbelief, etc.) are tested. We are being tested through our reactions and responses (our intentions and actions) to the tests we are exposed to.

Let's not forget that, since we have a limited view of the world (like someone said, we see the pixel, God sees the picture), we often assume something is evil, when it could lead to positive OR that something is good, when it could lead to disaster in the future. So, the very assessment of the condition could be faulty...

Due to our relative free will, man is capable of committing great acts of evil and injustice (i.e. driven by greed, racism, fear, and so on). However, a man who commits an evil act has committed a sin against his own soul, and the right of others, and will be judged accordingly.

God has not promised that we will experience a purely joyful life on this earth and die at a specific time and place! On the contrary, in the scripture we are informed that every soul will be tested with periods of plenty and misery and, ultimately, a taste of death. This is all in preparation for a future existence. No one will question God.

~

The super evil people of the world (serial killers etc.) are usually the product of some form of abandonment (or abuse) from their parents.

The vast majority of people, however, are capable of being both good or evil largely depending upon their environment. If you were born to a racist in the south in the past, you might gleefully watch an innocent black man being lynched and hanged. If that same person were raised in a non-racist environment instead, he would be appalled by the lynching. If you lived in Nazi Germany in the 30's, you might easily accept the genocide of Jews that occurred. If you were raised elsewhere, you would see that as horrific.

Also, the same person who gleefully watched the hanging or condoned the genocide, might later in life, with enough time spent in a moral environment, truly regret and feel horrible about their previous attitudes. Most humans are malleable.

As far as the large number of evil governments in the world (the cause of much pain and suffering), that is the unfortunate result of the tendency of many of the super-evil people I first talked about, to be driven toward power and sadly, often through intimidation, obtain that power. I can guarantee you that Hitler, Saddam Hussein, Stalin etc. all had abusive and/or psychologically abandoning parents (as do most serial killers). It is sad that they are able to rise to power but their sociopathy permits them to rise to power in many vulnerable countries through fear and killing off the opposition.

One latent characteristic that resides in many people is a characteristic that often tips the balance towards their embracing evil and is often exploited by an evil leader. That characteristic is racism (including religious bigotry). It is far easier for a Hitler to get a nation to embrace genocide when the impetus comes from racism. We are now seeing that even in a civilized country like America, a leader who feeds off of racism as does Trump, can get 40% of the country to accept horrific conduct such as ripping children out of the arms of their mothers.

The arc of history seems to slowly bend towards human decency. Not long ago in this country, thousands would show up to cheer public hangings which seems unthinkable now. The evolution of that arc, however, is slowed by the seemingly genetic trait in many people, to hate people of other races. We are currently seeing this phenomenon rear its ugly head not only in America but throughout the world. Hopefully in America at least, the racism that Trump has inflamed is the last gasp of that phenomenon, but it might be a very long gasp.

~

The Tarantula Hawk is a species of wasp. It is large, 2 to 3 times the size of regular wasps. It finds its prey, the tarantula, in the desert flying around and scanning. It then stings the tarantula and the big hairy spider is paralyzed from the venom. Tarantula Hawk then descends to the ground and drags the immobilized arthropod back to its nest. I would imagine this takes quite some time. At this point the wasp lays it eggs in the living tarantula and it acts as an incubator. The babies hatch and I would imagine the tarantula's usefulness has expired at this stage.

I watched a video of wolves. One pack was raiding another pack that had infringed on its territory. They killed the mom and then ate the babies.

"Horrible" things are happening in nature all the time. If a human behaved as the wolves or wasp, it would be judged differently. We can look at all the creatures, great and small, eating and preying on one another and see a natural order of "bad" things happening. I do not give humans a pass like I do wildlife since we are more complicated than the other creatures, at least in the complexity of our collective modus operandi. Our particular "bad" things come mostly from us and our behavior. I can't think of another species that has such capacity for bad intent as humans.

But maybe I'm being subjective. Maybe humans' behavior is just the same as the wolf or the wasp. We are a part, though a strange one, of nature too. So our behavior could be considered "natural". By the same reasoning an automobile or styrofoam container can be called natural. So is what we call "bad" just "what is" and we are qualifying it as such? Yes and also no. I still think the line is drawn between humans and other creatures because we knowingly cause "bad" and when the animals do it is just what they do with no evil intent.

So I guess bad things happen because some people are bad. I think it is a small percentage of people. The ones who cause speed bumps to be installed and park benches to be locked down.

~

Why do bad things happen? I think that life was created for an ultimate purpose and that evolution is one of the processes for accomplishing this. This process is accomplished through generations and generations of life – and requires death for everyone and much pain and suffering for everyone. Why? – if life didn't require competition for scarce resources, we wouldn't do whatever it takes to procreate as much possible. So I guess I think "bad things" are just a part of the mechanism which makes evolution possible – endless death, pain, extinctions, all serving the purpose of favoring survival traits and, I think a spark of group consciousness that is inevitably (or maybe not inevitably) heading toward some purpose. This seems pretty likely if you look at things from a longer perspective than just the last election cycle.

But what is it we are headed to? I don't know – my hopeful belief is that we will come to realize our dependency on each other and realize that God's kingdom is nowhere other than the here and now. Similarly, I don't think there is really a difference between pain and destruction caused by evil versus "acts of God". Humans have an immense capacity for violence, cruelty, self-centeredness, and rationalization for other peoples' pain and suffering. In fact, these characteristics are almost certainly favored by evolution. Genghis Khan, who died about 750 years ago is estimated to have 16 million male descendants alive today. Here's a quote attributed to Genghis Khan:

"The greatest joy for a man is to defeat his enemies, to drive them before him, to take from them all they possess, to see those they love in tears, to ride their horses, and to hold their wives and daughters in his arms."

(See article in Discover Magazine at: http://blogs.discovermagazine.com/gnxp/2010/08/1-in-200-men-direct-descendants-of-genghis-khan)

To me it's a wonder that despite being descendants of warlords, rapists, conquerors, and enslavers, we have discovered quantum physics, the theory of relativity, Johann Sebastian Bach, Emmy the Great, the Tao De Jing, Green Chile cheeseburgers, Tequila, and Better Call Saul.

But, I think we are at an important point - to some degree we have figured out how to stop the natural process of evolution – through advances in medicine, declining reproduction rates by those historically considered to be genetically favored, and by increasing barriers to "survival of the fittest."

Responses to Question 2: What does the next incarnation of conscious life look like to you when you try to imagine it?

~

Since this future version of intelligent life would likely be unaware of our previous existence, they would not have the benefit of learning from our mistakes? So they would probably recreate many of our mistakes. I don't think it will be Silurian Reptiles. Since earth is ¾ water, perhaps it would be a water-based life form-perhaps octopi? I've read that octopi are highly intelligent. They have the ability to manipulate thinks so they could "build stuff." But they are solitary animals and I think one of the definitions of a civilization requires community and communication? So perhaps communal octopi? Another option, because they are already here and already communal, could be one of the colony insects?

Perhaps sentient bees or ants or termites? Perhaps since they are much smaller, it is possible that they will cause less damage to our planet? This is an interesting question because, based on the number of plants and animals going recently extinct, many scientists feel we are now right in the midst of this sixth mass extinction. Edward Osbourne Wilson (coincidently, his specialty is myrmecology-the study of ants) predicts that 50% of mammals will be extinct by the year 2100. I read that in

November, a group of over 15,000 scientists issued a statement saying that already "we have unleashed a mass extinction event, the sixth in roughly 540 million years, wherein many current life forms could be annihilated or at least committed to extinction by the end of this century."

For more check out: http://eowilsonfoundation.org/

~

For this question I would say that I have no idea where humans will go next. My whimsical response comes from a classic Star Trek Episode (Original Series) "Errand of Mercy". Summary: in that episode in order to stop the violence between the Federation and The Klingon Empire on the planet Organia, the Organians disarm both sides. The climax of the episode reveals the truth about the Organians. Organians are millions of years beyond the need for physical bodies. They have evolved into advanced and powerful energy beings, and the outward appearance of Organia was solely to provide points of reference for visitors. The characters Ayelborne and Claymare disappear, turning into very bright pure energy. Maybe (hopefully?) that is the ultimate form the human race may take in some millions of years.

~

In one sense, I don't think we are anything especially special – if you told me that we are essentially malevolent creatures and in fact are the devil (that we invented to be something other than ourselves), I would be hard-pressed to defend my species.

But I would anyway.

When I was a kid, one of the stories my Dad read to us was *The Devil and Daniel Webster*. In this story, Daniel Webster stakes his soul to save a fellow New Hampshirian who has sold his soul to the devil. Daniel Webster has to convince a jury consisting of the worst people in human history (at least at that point in history), including Edward Teach (Blackbeard) with John Hathorne, who presided over the Salem Witch trials, as the judge. For whatever reason, this story cemented itself in my mind when I read this question about an extinction of the human race.

I would want to make the case for humans...

I would first argue that we are what we are – none of us participated in how we were created or how we evolved. So we are here now and we have gotten here through ruthlessness, destruction, and other terrible deeds.

Second, while the vast majority of us through history have been focused mostly on the daily struggles of life, which includes trying to get ahead of brothers and sisters either legally or illegally, morally or immorally, we have managed to create some amazing things in science, ways of thinking (philosophy, religion, and morality), codes to promote the development of society (language, laws, etc.).

~

Wow. I guess I brought it up, but really don't have an answer. Just some thoughts.

First of all, it is difficult to imagine humans being completely gone. I think that even if there is a massive die off of people, some will survive somewhere. In a future where some humans survive I think it will be much like any number of science fiction scenarios. There are many and they are ever expanding along with the development of technology. These futuristic notions become seemingly ever more plausible. I think these sci-fi ideas could be the subject of a whole other discussion.

If I am to imagine that all humans are dead and what the next "intelligent" life looks like. . .wow. Not easy. If no humans, then another surviving species would have to evolve.

This would take time. If we destroy ourselves through climate, then perhaps the world will be a toxic swamp of the most invasive and undesirable, ugly creatures for a while, and eventually the not-so-primordial soup would produce something. Maybe our artificial intelligence robots would continue on and the intelligent life would be machine based. Or cyborgs. Maybe something new would show up from the stars. Intelligent life or spores, who knows.

I must confess, I have yet to read the Post article on the possibility of intelligent life on earth before us. Though I helped raise this question, I find it vexingly difficult to answer in any way. I guess it is something that I just think of and wonder about.

My feeling about the future is that there are big changes ahead, already gradually happening. A lot of it will be dystopian and bizarre. Yet, I think there will be (of necessity) surprises. I hold some hope for the possibility of an unexpected use of a technology, or development of a new one, that will improve things on a wide scale, rapidly, and in unforeseen ways.

~

There is lots of life on this planet right now that is intelligent and will not leave a fossil record. Dolphins, octopi, and crows are all very intelligent. I think what you are asking is if there were any advanced civilizations on this planet before humans. I would think not for the reason that we have never seen any proof of communities or civilizations. While may not have been not be a fossil record, there would be buried debris, ruins, structures, made objects, etc that we would have found. So, I think that there have been intelligent species on this planet that did not leave a tangible trace, I think we are the first ones that created an advanced social structure and advanced civilization. I think the difference between being an intelligent species and an advanced civilization is the ability to communicate and learn from past experiences on a generational level; in other words, humans have been building and passing on knowledge for thousands of generations, each one building on the last. We have found no record of another species that has done that.

~

My thought is more about how humans may continue to evolve (rather than how an entirely new species might arise after an extinction). The physicist, Alan Lightman, has suggested that homo sapiens is moving toward homo techno. Already, highly sophisticated non-animate body parts are being implanted into human bodies. Perhaps it's not unreasonable to think that the technology that is now external may in the future become internal (e.g., accessing the internet simply by "thinking"). Humans would become an inextricable mix of animate and non-animate and philosophers will have to expand the definition of what it means to be "human".

ROUND 8: *SO, WHAT HAVE WE LEARNED SO FAR?*

Here was the prompt for the final round:

So, it is time to wrap this up: What HAVE you learned over the past year we have been working on this project? Please review our shared results so far (see attached) and if possible, reference an idea, thought, or a quote in our document as well as other experiences in the last year. Consider writing it as a note to a great great grandchild or to an intelligent being after the 6th extinction. What would you want them to know?

For rounds 1-7, I propose to keep all responses anonymous. For the last round (this one), I propose, with each person's express permission, to include your first name and last initial. *¡Adelante y hacia arriba!*

~

It has become so meaningful to me to sit with these questions posed throughout the year and ponder on what it is that I do believe. Certainly, the big questions have been put out there...the purpose of existence, suffering, death, transformation, the future, etc. I want to stress that my views are not only a work in progress but also, I am so aware, limited to my own experiences (much like the metaphor of the blind men trying to describe an elephant). That's why I think a conversation, like this one that Paul has initiated, is just what is needed. We can all add our own perspectives and our views can then broaden and expand. That said, slowly and haltingly I realize that I do believe in...

The beginning and the end for me is that I do believe in God (the One with many names) and that belief infuses and animates all that follows. I believe that we live in an evolving universe, one suffused with meaning and evolving in the direction of greater consciousness (Teilhard de Chardin). Since all creation comes from the same Source it necessarily follows that all creation is profoundly connected (St Francis and his brother Sun, etc.). We are all truly in this together. The deep interconnection of life is rapidly being expounded by scientists (e.g., our internal microbiome that has joined with us since birth and without which we now could not exist). And Love is the energy force that propels us forward toward ever greater unity and differentiation. To hate/destroy/resent others would mean hating myself. Another's suffering is my suffering. Another's success is my success too. There is a curious both/and quality to how I think we should proceed in life. On the one hand, we really need "do" nothing in order to be of infinite value. Evolution/Life/God created me, not the other way around, and I can deeply trust in that Process. I more need not to impede, not get in the way, not push the river. We can't make things happen through muscular effort or brute force. That being said, I also believe that everything that we do does matter. We must act with love and hope and faith and gratitude. We must seek justice for all and resist the powerful forces of racism (all "isms") and fear and violence. But I think I am advocating for acting without being overly attached to the results. The end does not justify the means, rather the means determine the result.

I really struggled (and still do) with the question of suffering. How could a loving and omnipotent God allow pain? How can it be that a baby can be born into a life that will be both brutal and short? I very tentatively grapple with the idea that perhaps God is evolving too...that we are born with the purpose of being co-creators...that we are needed in a very real way to live a life that serves the purpose of making the world what it needs to be and become.

One contributor referenced, "Be the change you are waiting for." Beautiful thought. One image I have of "my place" in the world is that of a tiny tile with a particular shape and color that is unique to me. Although I can't see the completed whole, I believe that my piece fits into the cosmically large mosaic/art that is composed of all creation. What is mine to do then is to live fully the particularity that is me (my longings, my talents, what makes my heart "leap"). Just as I need not/ must not conform wholly to external expectations, I must also support and encourage others to develop an awareness of their own singularity and soul's purpose. My sense of what is "true" evolves more from my experiences in trying to live in loving community than from rules taught from above. My groping for truth is more bottom-up than top-down (although I also believe that children need to socialized in the expectations of our culture. Later they can choose to reject what they have been taught, but at least they know what it is that they are rejecting.) Our culture, like every culture, has an ideology that gives direction and shape to our lives, but we must be aware that truth suffers whenever doors are closed and certainties prevail. As counter-intuitive as it seems, I believe that we must learn to hold seeming opposites with gentle attention rather than fully endorse one side and condemn the other. Martin Buber expresses it well.

"Fate and freedom are promised to each other. Fate is encountered only by him that actualizes freedom. That I discovered the deed that intends me, that, this movement of my freedom, reveals the mystery to me. But this, too, that I cannot accomplish it the way I intended it, this resistance also reveals the mystery to me. He that forgets all being caused, as he decides from the depths, he that puts aside possessions and cloak and steps bare before the Countenance - this free human being encounters fate as the counter-image of his freedom. It is not his limit but his completion; freedom and fate embrace each other to form meaning; and given meaning, fate - with its eyes, hitherto severe, suddenly full of light - looks like grace itself."

~

Somehow, I feel like I have not learned anything. Or that *"The only thing I know for sure is that I know nothing."* Sure, I've learned some new tangible things related to repairs, function, tools, plants and gardening, etc. But I don't think that is the kind of "learning" we have been writing about in this project. Thus, I have a hard time encapsulating it within the timeframe of one year.

This project has stimulated me to think about the questions it raises even more than I usually do. Which brings me back to kinds of learning. I think the kind of learning we are interested in is a continual process in which we don't exactly learn, but rather that things reveal themselves to us. We then have more of the picture. It isn't an entirely passive process though. We must put ourselves into an appropriate and receptive state. Then, I think it starts with questions and actively thinking, then finding the next question(s) followed by more thinking and careful observation. I see it as a life-long practice or meditation. A jigsaw puzzle with one million pieces that are all black. The complete picture will eventually manifest itself as what appears to be nothing.

One of the most important questions is from round one. Why are we here? Is there purpose? I asked what are we? This is one area where we can apply this "continuing learning meditation" to. I suppose it could apply to all our questions! Even the tangible things. After years of servicing and repairing the same kinds of equipment one can practically know immediately what the issue is at any given job. But every once in a while, said equipment behaves in mysterious and unorthodox ways. After figuring out what is going on I say to myself, "*Huh, I didn't know that could happen.*" We must not get complacent and think that we know everything there is to about something.

Plato's idea was that all learning is but a process of recollection. That we are born knowing all and spend our lives "recollecting" it, due to the soul's necessary amnesia from being born an infant. To me this resonates with the continual process/practice/meditation idea.

In "The Hitchhikers Guide to the Galaxy" (there's 5 books in the "trilogy", rest in peace Douglas Adams) a supercomputer is built to figure out the answer to "life, the universe, and everything". Spoiler alert, after a vast amount of time the computer finds the answer to be "42". The greatly disappointed people are told by the machine that perhaps they didn't ask the right question. Maybe we should seek the questions more than answers. Kind of like "the journey is the destination".

I think this quote points to what I struggle to describe with words the best. It is also from "Ghost Dog, The Way of the Samurai" soundtrack.

Samurai Code Quote #6
"Our bodies are given life from the midst of nothingness.
Existing where there is nothing is the meaning of the phrase "form is emptiness".

That all things are provided for by nothingness is the meaning of the phrase "emptiness is form".
One should not think that these are two separate things."

~

I took this last round very seriously and even did the homework. I picked out some of the things that people mentioned as the resources that spoke to them and watched, read, listened and pondered. I watched '*Happy*' and '*Accidental Courtesy*' on Netflix. I listened to Bach, especially Suite #3 in D Major. I was already a fan of '*Little Wing*' but everyone knows that the best Alison Krauss song is '*Forget About It*'. I am also a huge Handel's Messiah fan and listened to it again while writing this. I love Nina Simone. If you do too, and if you have the opportunity, see the play "Nina Simone: Four Women,". It was recently at Arena stage and it was an experience. I have read several of the books referenced on the banned book list and I am committed to going out of my way to read/re-read more of them in my future readings. I plan to enjoy them just a little more knowing they are on someone's list as being morally objectionable. I think reading and listening to other people's favorite things is an important way to evolve your world view and I appreciated everyone's suggestions! In the immortal words of Jimmy Buffett:

"As a dreamer of dreams and a travelin' man,
I have chalked up many a mile.
Read dozens of books about heroes and crooks,
And I've learned much from both of their styles."

To answer the question of what we have learned so far, here are some of my thoughts:

1. Someone somewhere along the way said: *"Maybe the point here is that we should live to create God's kingdom on earth and should have an immediacy to it..."*

   I agree and harkening back to the first two segments of the exercise, I've evolved my purpose in life answer. I think that the way to achieve the 'kingdom of heaven' and to achieve our purpose is to strive to be happy. Happiness seems like a very simple concept, but it is actually very complex and maybe even a little bit difficult to quantify and define.

   Many people in our group agreed that an aspect of feeling purposeful and happy centered around doing for others, getting over yourself, focusing on community and helping others. From the Netflix show "Happy" they talked about people finding fulfillment by being in a 'zone'. Examples of people being in their zone included surfing and other types of physical activity. They also referenced people playing music and even provided examples of people whose jobs were opportunities to be in their 'zone'. Being in the zone equates to being so perfectly focused on an activity that you can tune out all other distractions/worries and be in the moment with your activity. This results in increased levels of dopamine being released and leads to people feeling happy. Another piece of being happy seems to be taking time to focus on the blessings in your life rather than focusing on what is bad about your life.

   I really like this formula for happiness and so my guidance to the next generations/worlds would be to invest themselves in being happy. I think that is my guidance to myself and those around me too. Actively look for things that put you in your 'zone'. Make time every day to do those things. Always be on the look-out for new things that put you in your zone. Try to help people out as much as you possible. No matter what you have going on, it always makes you feel good when you help others. Focus on the great things in life! It is important to put time and mental energy into enjoying the simplest things in life like a great meal, a nice beer, a warm bed, a deep conversation, the moment when you know the band is playing your favorite song at the concert, a great book/movie/tv show, something to laugh hard about. People get caught up thinking that happiness comes from complex things I don't think it is true.

2. I would hope for society in the next generation/next world to take the phrase '*There but for the grace of God go I*' (or equivalent) to heart when evaluating their opinions on things. Just because you are not personally experiencing: poverty, living in a world without medical insurance, racism, being sexually harassed, unemployment, addiction, living on food stamps, living in a place that isn't safe with a desire to find a place where your children are safe, etc. doesn't mean you are absolved of responsibility for having compassion, understanding and options to help people who are. Modern society and future society can benefit from this concept.

3. When you see Nazi's marching down the street in Charlottesville it is really easy to become discouraged, disillusioned, despondent about our world. Resist the urge to let the bad people around you drag you down to their level of darkness. As Martin Luther King, Jr. said *"Darkness cannot drive out darkness; only light can do that. Hate cannot drive out hate; only love can do that."*

    I don't think we all have the ability to talk sense into closed minded people (like Daryl Davis – the guy featured in Accidental Courtesy), but we can all have faith in society to evolve. We can all 'model the behavior' - act in the ways we hope others will also act. Giving into despair isn't the answer.

And to end how I started, I will sum it all up with a Jimmy Buffett quote:

"some of it's magic, some of it's tragic,
But I had a good life all the way"

~

I admit that I have not been keeping up with this, even though I love this idea. I really wish that I had been able to contribute responses, but I know that each time I received an email, I just thought "I need to finish my lab report first" or "I'll do this when I'm less stressed and have a clearer mind." But it occurs to me now that the point of WHWLSF is to take a step back from our busy lives and really think about ourselves and how we fit into the world and universe around us. I don't mean to say that I spent 4 years pouring over textbooks and problem sets without ever thinking about anything deep. My absolute best memories of college are the ones shared with new friends in which we talked about many of the very topics I am now discovering are in WHWLSF. It is amazing to consider that we have our own deep and meaningful personal opinions on things, and then realize that every other human being we encounter has their own sets of opinions. It is unfortunate that we don't usually get to share our thoughts or hear the thoughts of others on a normal basis. For some reason we seem to need an event, the help of some substance, or a guide to share our most important thoughts with others. It occurs to me that I don't even know these opinions of all of my family members or close friends, when those opinions are kind of the most important and defining ones. Why do we care what sports team someone roots for, and yet we don't care whether they think there is a purpose to our lives?? I think interacting with people would be a lot more enjoyable and meaningful if it was socially acceptable to ask these sorts of questions from the beginning. Additionally, we would be exposed to many more ideas which would aid in our collectively human understanding of ourselves and the universe.

Maybe I am just in that place in my life where I am afraid of a future after college, but I am genuinely going to miss the 2 AM conversations with a group of equally-confused young adults on the meaning of life over a crappy bottle of 7-11 wine. It seems to me that these sorts of conversations are going to become less and less frequent as I get older, and that scares me. In the "real world" it looks like everyone is so wrapped up in their daily lives and politics that there isn't any time or energy left to think or discuss important ideas. WHWLSF has made me more aware of the people around me and their opinions. I am making a personal note of asking every friend I run into today their opinions on some of these questions, even though it's probably not what I would normally do.

So, I did ask a few friends for their opinions and as usual, they thought it was a bit weird at first. But once one person shared their ideas, a conversation sparked and people couldn't shut up. I asked them if they wished they could ask or be asked those sorts of questions more frequently, and I got responses such as, "Yeah, you don't really know a person too well until you do," "Yes, I could have figured out my ex's true colors a lot faster," and "Yeah, these conversations are a lot more interesting than bullshitting about stuff that isn't important." The general consensus was that they liked it.

Why exactly DO we feel good when we talk to other people about important issues? I think it lets us take a break from our everyday busy lives that focus on relatively boring and routine things, and instead focus on something that unites us all together. We all know that feeling where we start at a new school or new job, and we're desperate to make any connection with the new people around us. We crave that feeling of having something in common with other people, and in those types of situations, finding out that someone else also watches Game of Thrones can feel like you've now signed a pact saying you two are bonded for eternity. But something as simple as a shared interest in Game of Thrones can't possibly compare to a shared interest in the role and fate of humanity and the universe! These conversations let us hear what other people believe and incorporate the ideas we like into our own beliefs. It's cool to think that each person has their own unique belief (finger) print that has been weathered by life experiences and other people. Maybe one day, if everyone were keener on sharing and learning other beliefs, we'd be a lot closer to finding out the truth (if there is just one truth).

I think another thing that can help shape our beliefs is creativity. I think "you are so creative!" is one of the absolute best compliments to receive. When I was little, I used to think being creative meant you just think of random things at random times. My little mind struggled with that- I didn't think you could be creative if you were *trying* to be creative, because then it's not random. I think there is still an inherent nature to creativity, but now I think that you can absolutely grow your creativity through exercising your brain and experiencing things that aren't typical for you. People say that JK Rowling must have had an extreme amount of creativity to write the Harry Potter books, which is definitely true. But she didn't just spontaneously think up all the concepts from the books- she had a lot of inspiration from Lord of the Rings and tons of other literature. That doesn't discount her creativity- I think she was able to be so creative with her writing because she had already expanded her mind. The same thing goes for Harry Potter readers. Anyone who reads those books has now expanded their mind a little bit to consider the fantastic and magical ideas JK Rowling wrote about. And then maybe some will go on to write even more bizarre books!

It might be easier to think about in the scientific community. Back when no one knew anything, we had a very small circle of knowledge. As discoveries happened, the "scientific knowledge bubble" expanded and expanded. Nowadays, we (as a society) don't have to go through the whole process of discovering that the Earth is round or that living things have cells for ourselves because thankfully people in the past did that for us. So we get to start life early on with a bigger bubble of knowledge. Today, it's impossible to know everything in the scientific knowledge bubble. That's why we have specialists and scientists who are top in their field to call upon if we want to know something or get a different perspective. Maybe if we thought about creativity and our knowledge of human fate like we do about a "scientific knowledge bubble," we'd see the value in sharing our ideas. We won't get anywhere if we don't explore the beliefs of others. I am grateful for WHWLSF for making me remember the importance of deep thinking and sharing of opinions. I think this is a great way for people to share their ideas, and hopefully this inspires people to be more mindful and willing to talk about deep opinions with others in their daily lives.

~

I was raised as a Methodist and attended church, regularly throughout my youth. However, as I continued my education and became a social scientist I became much more of a believer in an evidence-based approach to life. So, I would describe myself today as an agnostic. I am willing to believe in God and an afterlife but I rely on evidence that I can perceive with my senses. I do not consider myself an atheist. In fact, the more I learn about science the more it seems to violate the rules of what we can perceive with our evidence-based faculties! I am especially amazed by my nonprofessionals' understanding of quantum physics and some of the counter intuitive extrapolations being made in this area. If it turns out that the world is being run by a God and her/his earthly image is with robes, long hair and sandals it would hardly be more surprising than string theory.

In contemplating this issue I almost started by writing that I consider myself agnostic because I cannot claim that God talks to me. I did not write that though because sometimes I am not so sure—mostly when surrounded by great natural beauty it sometimes feels to me like there must be a Divine. But then I look at what we know of life in our universe—where we appear to be stranded on a not very distinguished or unusual rock that is not in the center of anything but in a kind of odd pocket in an odd pocket in the galaxies. I am told that there are most likely many other similar rocks scattered about the universe—and most likely some of them also contain life. So, it could be that the Jews, or Christians or Muslims or Buddhists are right—or it could be that in reality we are only some crazy science experiment and right now our entire universe is sitting in some intelligent being's great petri dish, perched on their kitchen table. I am in no position to know the difference. I guess I would describe myself as a "naturalist." I try to interpret the world I live in through the natural senses that I have. In biblical terms, I am an avowed "doubting Thomas."

It does seem remarkably sad to me that I will one day die. And without a belief in an afterlife it is also very sad to me that once dead, I will no longer be able to see the people I have loved and those who have loved me. On the other hand, this realization gives life an incredible sweetness. I am reminded of the Anne Rice vampire books—where vampires—who can live forever—eventually commit suicide because it is just too damned difficult to keep changing with the times. Being around forever would raise its own challenges.

I am mixed on the topic of whether religion is a good thing or a bad thing. From an evolutionary standpoint I am guessing that it must be a good thing or it would not persist. In fact, the architects of the modern social sciences—Durkheim, Comte, Marx, Weber—all predicted that religion would fade away and be replaced by science. That certainly has not happened!

Would the world be a better place without religion—as in the John Lennon song "Imagine?" Religion certainly has good features. Compared to the non-religious, religious people have more of what social scientists call "social capital." They are more likely to contribute to the welfare of others. They have more children. Lower divorce rates. Less crime. I imagine they probably live longer. In the US, the highly religious state of Utah often finishes near the top on fertility and civic engagement and near the bottom on crime and poverty. On the other hand, religion can be harnessed for bad behavior and even violence. As we have seen in recent years through groups like al Qa'ida and ISIS, when religion is harnessed for a cosmic purpose, it can be quite deadly.

I would guess that on balance religion continues because compared to non-religious societies, religious societies have more kids and are better at raising them to adults. From the Mormons to the Muslims, strongly religious societies tend to have high rates of fertility.

What would the world look like without religion? It might look a lot like the European Union! Church attendance in the countries of the EU has dropped to extremely low levels. So that we have the situation where the great cathedrals of Europe have relatively few active members. The decline in religion among Europeans is no doubt one of the flashpoints

in terms of the current battle over immigration in Europe—
where you have basically non-religious Europeans being con-
fronted with highly religious immigrants from the Middle
East, Africa and elsewhere.

But one must ask where do we get ethics and morality from
if not from religion? Certainly, I feel like I got my basic sense
of right and wrong from my early upbringing in church. Without religion, what is the basis for treating others with respect
or some version of the "golden rule." I am not sure about this
one. I don't see how science can directly answer that question.
I believe that Germany was one of the most scientifically sophisticated countries in the world just before they pivoted into
support for the Nazis. Can we construct a non-religious version
of morality and ethics? This seems to me to be a worthy challenge. And there are certainly plenty of examples where highly
religious societies have done awful things to others. And also
examples, like contemporary Scandinavia, where essentially
non-religious societies are treating most of their citizens with
respect and dignity.

~

What a terrific project this has been for me! I think we are
hard-wired to search for answers to questions to the big questions. To some extent, we can't find the answers. The process
is probably more important – you can't answer the questions,
but you can live a more purposeful life. The search is mostly
a solitary pursuit, but it sure was nice to think these questions
through with this group.

So, here are some of my summary thoughts:

1. **We are not individual souls, egos, individual con-
   sciousnesses.** I think the concept of self, and its inevitable result of selfishness are a necessary element of

evolution and it has gotten us this far, but we will need to realize our oneness and obligations to each other to move forward and even to survive. I think that Einstein's quote captures this:

> *"A human being is a part of the whole called by us universe, a part limited in time and space. He experiences himself, his thoughts and feeling as something separated from the rest, a kind of optical delusion of his consciousness. This delusion is a kind of prison for us, restricting us to our personal desires and to affection for a few persons nearest to us. Our task must be to free ourselves from this prison by widening our circle of compassion to embrace all living creatures and the whole of nature in its beauty."*

2. **The universe and existence is not linear, it's circular and overlapping.** I believe the barriers of time, distance, big and small, are illusions. The mention of the video "Powers of Ten" at the Air and Space museum and the metaphor of the Ouroboros triggered my thoughts on this idea.

3. **The images of our relationship to each other and to God as a mosaic or a painting are the best metaphors that I can think of.** We are all parts of the mosaic, and if we could step back we would see/know "meaning" or the face of God. I think that this metaphor is best described by the concept of Pantheism. It's probably impossible, or close to impossible (how can a mosaic tile step out of the mosaic and "see" the image?). Still I think we can get glimpses of the image if we live a purposeful life and keep our eyes open to meaning/mystery. This concept of us and God or us and our relationship, which I think is best described by the concept of pa-

nentheism, to the universe has other important implications, I think:

- The concepts of original sin, evil, shame, hell, karma, guilt are illusions. We are children of God, in God's image and likeness, and even a part of God. Like any parent, God loves us unconditionally, and if we could step back and look at the mosaic, it is perfect. This doesn't explain why bad things happen and why people are cruel, but I think it's still "true".
- In a sense, there's nothing we need to "do". We are created for a purpose. We don't need to know our purpose, we are already accomplishing it. Reconciling my desire and sense of urgency to solve the mysteries and live my life better with this Daoist concept of inaction and effortlessness is something I would like to get better at (recognizing that this is a contradiction).

4. **The Kingdom is right here, right now**. We should live as if there is no afterlife, no god, and no purpose. I particularly liked the thoughts of the team members who do not believe in an afterlife and who are agnostic. Round 3 (on death) seemed to be the topic of most interest to the group. I believe that nobody really knows what happens after we die and we should be compelled to live our lives as if there's nothing after. If we live our lives purposefully, with no expectation of a punishment or reward, we will leave calmly, contently, and happy. That's my plan anyway. It's what I think John Lennon meant by "*Imagine there's no heaven*" – not that it doesn't exist, just that it shouldn't affect how we decide to live.

Taking the idea that the kingdom is right here and right now, means that we have a sacred responsibility to "make" it the kingdom is should be. And that responsibility is to focus on ourselves, not to change others. I think the notion of *"change yourself and you change the world"* is right and a powerful concept. Or as Belinda Carlisle sings, *"Ooh Heaven is a place on earth."*

5. **Writing may be the closest we can get to the truth.** After participating in the project for this past year, I have realized the amazing power that writing has to contemplate and have insights into the mystery of why we are here and what we're supposed to do. I think reading and writing are the closest things we have to the magical. What I only came to know in this past year is how act of writing stimulates the mind in such a different way than the passive act of reading. I don't fully comprehend the meaning of the haunting beginning of the gospel of St. John: *"In the beginning was the word, and the word was with God, and the word was God"* but I think it means that ideas, articulated in words that are written down and passed on to others through time, have an existence of their own, some type of consciousness, an ability to create a universe from nothing. I think that the Japanese word *"Kotodama"* describes this concept. I want to learn more about this idea.

I really think that the concept of this collaborative writing project combines several of these above things: 1) we exist in context of each other, 3) we can only see the "face of God" by abandoning our self-focus, 4) there is an immediateness to our lives – do it now, not later, and writing as a way of heading toward truth.

I'll finish this essay with a quote that by Ray Bradbury: *"Let the world burn through you. Throw the prism light, white hot, on paper."*

~

I think there is a purpose to our lives. I think living things are biologically wired to have a "purpose". For many living things, the purpose is to survive long enough to reproduce and pass on genetic information. There are several species that display this "selflessness" quite clearly. I remember learning about octopus mothers, who take care of their eggs for large amounts of time. By the time the eggs hatch, she is too starved and spent to survive - a "mother who could give nothing more".

http://phenomena.nationalgeographic.com/2014/07/30/octopus-cares-for-her-eggs-for-53-months-then-dies/

The prevalence of this purpose is quite obvious - obviously, a creature who is most adept at surviving and passing genetic information will survive and pass on its genetic information. Natural selection selects for these traits and if there were animals or plants or fungi that decided instead to pursue a different "purpose" in the world, it died without passing on its genetic information (but not before getting laughed at and shunned by its community).

Outside of the human species, it is difficult to find cases that defy this biological purpose. I've heard of dogs who sacrifice themselves for their owners, and plants who were distressed by the screams of boiling shrimp. Colonial behaviors in which some organisms appear to act "selfless" can be explained quite easily: the success of any one individual is enhanced when part of a community, even if the individual might from time to time need to perform activities without the direct purpose of spreading genetic information.

Then we come to humans: I've heard it argued that humans have transcended natural selection. What people mean by this is that with modern medicine, humans have managed to thwart the age old "survival of the fittest". In some ways this is true- we have care for the elderly and the disabled. Being smart or physically fit doesn't necessarily enhance a person's survival or ability to pass on genetic information, as it might have when humans first evolved. This is quite clear to me, as the person in arguably the most powerful position in the world right now is not young, smart, or physically fit. I wouldn't argue that natural selection has necessarily been "transcended", but I would go for a calmer "subdued".

Well, now that we don't have to worry about natural selection, and pretty much any idiot can reproduce, what do we do with ourselves? It is clear why humans are probably the only species to seek "purpose" other than the purpose dictated by nature. While having the time to think about these things is certainly a factor, I don't think it's the only factor. Yes, I am inside writing this email pondering the purpose of live, while the squirrels outside my house are too busy finding food in order to survive. But I don't think that if squirrels weren't busy surviving, that they'd be pondering philosophical questions (I could be wrong). Although I think that there is something to be learned from dogs: they've got it pretty easy, and what do they do with their time? Eat, nap, play. And repeat! I've never seen a dog having an existential crisis, but perhaps this is what living things would do if they weren't worried about surviving- they'd enjoy themselves and spend time with those that they love. I think that is a perfectly good place to start with "What is the purpose to our lives?"

Of course, you could also go the cat route: Eat, nap, knock things off counters, nap, and most importantly, nap.

However, I think the real reason humans seek purpose is not because we're bored but because we have the capacity. We have the most advanced nervous systems and are the only self-aware beings (that we know of). I've often thought about what makes us different from other living things, and this is it. There is an excellent documentary on Netflix that my dad showed me, called "Happy". It interviewed people all over the world, and asked them what it means to be happy, and why they are happy. It followed people who "shouldn't" be happy: some of the poorest people in the world, as well as people with extremely difficult lives and past experiences. These are people that do have to worry about survival on a daily basis, and yet seek more.

HOWEVER, the knowledge of our own knowledge, only makes me think about what we don't have the capacity to know. For example, if you were to stand and look at a plant on the forest floor, does the plant even know you're there and observing it? Probably not. Plants do have sensory capabilities, but they don't know much about something if it's not interacting with it in a way it understands.

What if we are a plant? And there is an alien species, or Eternal Being observing us? What if our search for "purpose" is as silly to them as a dog's purpose is to us? Professional philosophers with their heightened understanding of the world and turned-up noses know nothing more than "eat, nap, play". The point is, we do not know.

WE DO NOT KNOW!! If there is something more than us, we almost assuredly do not have the capacity to understand it or maybe even detect its presence. Now this seems like a ridiculous reason to believe there is something more, simply because we don't know that there isn't (Schrodinger had a similar hypothesis). But I'm not done!

While I don't believe we can fully grasp or understand "something more", I do think we can glimpse it, and I think everyone does. There are so many ways, I think it's impossible that any one way is the way. Now, I am a Catholic, and so can say I believe I have experienced glimpses of "greater than us" during particularly great homilies (very rare, I know), emotional retreats, great books, and late-night conversations.

I've also experienced glimpses outside of the Catholic church: reading Siddhartha, by Herman Hesse, talking to a Mormon friend, learning about other religions and thinking "Hey, this sounds familiar". So much of it makes sense, that I can't believe the Catholic church has is all - it is an earthly institution after all. I don't think anyone on earth has it all.

There are experiences beyond religion that I think are just as worthy: nature, laughing with friends, a really good meal, a great vacation, a snow day, waking up and thinking it's a weekday, but it's SATURDAY!

These are experiences that almost make your heart stop as you think, "this is perfect". But it's not quite perfect. You can never experience any of these experiences fully. Have you ever been at a concert, laughing with friends, sitting around a Christmas tree with your family, and thought "This is happiness. I wish it would never end." But it does end. It always does. Perhaps this is why we so ardently try to preserve these happy experiences- does a camera capture what you saw in nature? Does a grainy snapchat video capture the concert you went to? A group chat you made with your friends in high school as you vowed to stay in touch? None of it even comes close to the original.

And that is why I think we can never be perfectly happy on earth. I don't think its a worthless cause to seek temporary happiness, because memories can bring a smile on a bad day. But I can't stop thinking, there must be more.

When I watch a happy movie or a Youtube video where a child is reunited with a father that has been in Iraq, why does it make me cry?

I think it's because of an innate longing. A longing for more. Maybe that's why I then watch similar YouTube videos for the next couple of hours instead of doing homework. We long for things to be like that always. For things to be perfectly perfect, forever.

I think that I discovered this independently but was unable to put it into words until my eighth-grade religion class where we learned proofs for the existence of God. The scientific proofs, which I thought would appeal to me, left me unsatisfied. We studied Aquinas along with numerous philosophers. The only one that made sense to me was what I've written above. I'm sure it had a name and a philosopher attached to it, but they escape me. It bothers me to present an idea without attributing it to its source, and I will try to figure it out. Most likely it was C.S. Lewis or Peter Kreeft.

~

In order to respond to the request to supply just one more essay for the year-long project, I decided to read or reread the responses accrued since August 2017. Fascinating reading; it took much of the afternoon, because none of the submissions was exactly a "beach read." That's a good thing. My first reaction was something along these lines: Look at all these thoughts people are willing to share as anonymous! Bet we might be tighter lipped if we signed each one. But then again, I am grateful that people spent their precious time to articulate their thoughts on these topics. Now, each of us knows more or understands more about those in this particular circle. Thank you for this gift.

During the course of this year, I entered another decade of life. That often calls for an extra measure of introspection. What stands out for me is that the daily-ness of life can be complex and simple at the same time. It seems easier now to focus on goals; I am no longer eager to prove myself (shed that many years ago). That makes life a lot richer, believe it or not. Some of my beliefs from earliest times are still gripped firmly, such as: There is not nearly enough kindness in this world. So I still act on those beliefs in the same ways as I did way back when.

There really are such things as necessary losses in life, but it is truly painful to endure them. (See "Judith Viorst's book *Necessary Losses* for more insight.) Lost dreams, broken friendships, unfulfilling careers, demise of cherished parents or spouse, really can chip away at one's positive outlook. The truth of loss is that it is part of life. We fold it into what we feel and know and carry on.

Now, the origin of this project are several ponderous questions. We won't have the answers to life's biggest questions, I don't believe. (Maybe in the next life we shall learn more.) That will keep humans asking the same ones in perpetuity. That keeps us always seeking. To me that is a good thing, being a seeker. It takes courage, though.

Here is something I refer to from time to time. It was published in *Family Circle*, March 27, 1978, written by Nadine Stair of Kentucky:

"If I had my life to live over, I'd dare to make more mistakes next time. I'd relax, I would limber up. I would be sillier than I have been this trip. I would take fewer things seriously. I would climb more mountains and swim more rivers. I would eat more ice cream and less beans. I would perhaps have more actual troubles, but I'd have fewer imaginary ones.

You see, I'm one of those people who live sensibly and sanely hour after hour, day after day. Oh I've had my moments, and if I had it to do over again, I'd have more of them. In fact, I'd try to have nothing else. Just moments, one after the other, instead of living so many years ahead of each day. I've been one of those persons who never goes anywhere without a thermometer, a hot water bottle, a raincoat and a parachute. If I had to do it again, I would travel lighter than I have.

If I had my life to live over, I would start barefoot earlier in the spring and stay that way later in the fall. I would go to more dances. I would ride more merry-go-rounds. I would pick more daisies."

Nadine was 85 years of age when this was published.

As I wrote above, it takes courage.

⁓

Each question challenged me to put a halt to everyday chores and ponder the existential challenge from Paul. I was comforted knowing that the group allowed me complete freedom of thought exploration and no fear in sharing my musings with them. I loved letting each thought take me into another thought or at times, just hang there contemplating and circling a single idea before moving on.

Each month I looked forward to the reward when Paul sent out the summary of everyone's thoughts. It never ceased to amaze me how many ways the question was explored by others. Everyone had their own twist. The project never made me feel the need to critique someone's writings or to opine that I agreed or disagreed with them. I felt only joy in exploring someone else's introspection and contemplations.

So, in this era where extremists are taking over conversations, I thank Paul for reminding us that the exchange of ideas creates better more complete ideas.

⁓

I have thought about your question to the group and realized there were so many things I could say and there were many paths I could take in formulating a reply. While my treatment may be considered a narrow response to your broad question, I felt passionate about the topic.

As usual, a narrative came to me via one of the podcasts that I listen to from time to time. In this case, the podcast comes from Matt Fraud and is called "Pints With Aquinas". Matt begins each podcast with the opening "if you could sit down with the Angelic Doctor over a pint of beer, (Matt is Australian I think) and ask Thomas any question, what would it be?" Well the topic that intrigued me this time came in a podcast entitled: *Was there a real Adam & Eve?* The podcast content went way beyond that title and got into aspects of evolution, language development and science. The interview was conducted with Father Nicanor Austriaco, a Dominican priest/professor at Providence College. Fr. Austriaco is a remarkable person in that he has a Ph.D in Microbiology.

So my reply to your question...."Consider writing it as a note to a great great grandchild or to an intelligent being after the 6th extinction. What would you want them to know?" is as follows.

In our present day we are inundated with numerous opinions, theories, fame and fortune seekers and attention grabbers of all stripes on social media. Some of those offer reasoned opinions and theories and some offer unreasoned and extreme opinions. In Father's words, *"where do we find help in guiding us through the Class 5 rapids and safely avoid the rocks?"*

Fr. Austriaco said the we now live in an age of Fideism. One definition of Fideism is that Reason and Faith are hostile to each other and that Faith alone is the superior way to arrive at the truth.

At the end of the podcast Matt asked Fr. Austriaco to summarize along the lines of how to bring Faith and Reason together. What should I

What should I do? What do I listen to? Where do I begin? Fr. Austriaco's response was very intriguing. He is a Dominican, the same Order as Thomas Aquinas. His suggestion to bring Faith and Reason together was as follows.

1. Begin by reading Philosophy in the perennial tradition. (this is the view that each of the world's religious traditions share a single, metaphysical truth or origin from which all esoteric and exoteric knowledge and doctrine has grown.
2. Learn to talk and think about what is really real.
3. Humility is needed to be able to explain/understand things that are frequently not black and white. Be able to explain how we don't know what we don't know and that knowing how to explain how we know what we don't know is a way of explaining what we do know.

In Fr. Austriaco's view, Aquinas is the best way forward to do this, maybe in a group where people's minds are open to the opposition. (A method used by Aquinas was to raise the top five objections to a moral issue and then provide reasoned answers to those objections.) It was said Aquinas could argue the opposing position better than the opposition could. Therefore, Austriaco says to answer the opposition strive to be a better atheist than the atheist, be a better secular humanist than the secular humanist in an effort to lead them to Christ, the ultimate goal.

Take the example of any moral issue that may be plaguing you or raising doubts in your mind. Ask yourself (or learn to think) - how does this moral position jibe with the requisite science? Be sure to deal with only one issue at a time. There is too much out there and it is easy to get bogged down. Engage thoughtful experts in that particular field of thought. In other words get together with other disciplines in an effort to deal with all sides of the issue.

The message to a grandchild (or any sentient being from another dimension) is this. My take away is that on many troubling issues Faith and Reason, understood properly in their correct applications, should not be incompatible.

~

The following essay was published in WesleyNexus' January newsletter: http://wesnex.org/january-2018-newsletter/

What I Have Learned So Far by Rick Barr

Last summer, my good friend and audit colleague Paul Jackson sent me an email inviting me to participate in a project called "What you have learned so far where he requested that participants respond to the Templeton Foundation's "Big Questions": 1) Why are we here? 2) How Can We Flourish? 3) What is the Fundamental Structure of Reality? Since I have known Paul for 20 years, having worked with him as an auditor and having him participate in the IRAS discussion group, I was asked the simple question, what have I learned over the past 20 years? Simple? Not! So, I have procrastinated for a half year not knowing quite what to say. But it is a new year and time to start fresh and deliver on my well-intentioned but unfulfilled promise. So, what have I learned? As Paul pointed out in his initial invitation, getting the right question is half the problem. I think he is right on this but the question given was not quite right, at least for me. While I have learned a great deal over the past 20 years, I have forgotten much and also found that some of what I have learned was inaccurate, imprecise and, in some cases, likely false. In addition, many ideas are just plain beyond me (mathematical physics) and only accessible through third-party popular presentations. This is true in both science and, to a lesser degree, theology. For me, the question should not be what I have learned, or what I know or who I find most compelling but what fundamental concepts are deep enough, broad enough and promising enough to provide a grounding on how I understand the world. To focus more precisely, what ideas would I want to convey that would capture how I understand the world if I had only a 30 second elevator ride to do so? I have chosen four concepts that fit this bill. The four concepts I choose are novelty, emergence, personally engaged dialectic and beloved community. In my understanding, these concepts are all related to each other and provide clarification to each other. In 30 seconds, one can get only an inkling of what is meant, perhaps just a tease, but hopefully that is enough. So here is my elevator speech.

Too often we think of the world as governed by the laws of nature and certainly there are numerous patterns in nature that repeat and are subject to scientific inquiry. That is what science is all about and I affirm its findings. However, there are other aspects of our world which both transcends and works with these scientifically discerned patterns. Novelty, though hard to grasp conceptually and therefore too often dismissed, provides a complementary dimension to the discoveries of science. In novelty one encounters uniqueness, particularity and surprise. When contemplating novelty, one perceives the newness of processes and also their values. In my understanding, it is through embedded, on-going, incremental novelty that the qualitative complexities of our world arise. Over time, this novelty eventually leads to emergence of new, unanticipated patterns. In the science and religion dialogue, this emergence of qualitative complexity provides the layers of depth which are so important to this interdisciplinary enterprise. To begin to understand this depth, however, one cannot be wedded to a single methodology or discipline but instead must engage dialectically across the numerous conceptual and experiential landscapes with other participants. This is what I mean by engaged dialectic. This engagement needs to be open, personal and humble with participants willing to adjust their own ideas and beliefs based on the insights of others. It also requires a commitment to the ongoing discovery of truth and the correction of error in a never-ending process of interpretation. As the philosopher Josiah Royce stated, "*The world is a progressively realized community of interpretation*" or, in short, what he called "*the Beloved Community.*" It is in this community that truth and meaning can be found.

So that is my elevator speech, not an argument and not a proof but a short entree into what I have been able to perceive as both important and real coming from two decades of immersion in science and religion. It also provides a means of interpreting the Christian message, the ongoing tasks of Christian living and the engagement with persons from other faiths or no faiths at all. I doubt any readers agree with me fully but that is where I would want to begin. That is where the conversation starts.

WRAP-UP (FOR NOW)

So that's what we came up with! I am so grateful for this team of intrepid collaborators who stuck through this thinking and writing project. I had a vague idea of what I wanted to do and over the year this group played along. I think, to some extent, we created something new.

At least for me, this writeup contains more meaning than just about anything I have read or learned before (except for Victor Frankl's amazing book of course) because it includes the wisdom of people who I personally know, respect, and look up to, and the results draw and build upon what the others shared.

And partly because these collaborators knew that this was important to me, they took the time to share what they learned with me, with each other, and anyone who has happened upon this write-up.

So, what's next? Most of this team have said they want to do another collaborative writing project and I do too. So we will and I am excited about that. But, there are two other things that I want to do that came out of this experience.

First, I think the concept of collaborative thinking and putting "ink to paper" is a powerful idea. Maybe it is a way to create the bridges we need to move forward in a society where: (1) people are seemingly headed quickly toward division and enmity and disassociation from alternative views and, (2) technology and the marketing industry's increased and relentless promotion of consumerism over personal connection and delayed gratification that is essential to personal development of the species.

If our society was a marriage, it would be headed for a bad ending if we don't find a better way of dialogue.

Secondly, there was one theme over this past year that hit me over and over – the idea that we have created a culture that increasingly allows us to live in our bubbles and interact and socialize with people with almost identical and self-reinforcing views.

These bubbles enhance a basic human characteristic that allows us to see the faults in others and not our own. We see idiots, racists, sexists, misogynists in others and not own narrow-mindedness and ignorance. After I call someone a racist because of who they voted for or because I have a different view on an issue, I have eliminated the opportunity to ever have a meaningful dialogue with that person.

We should call out truth against injustice and intolerance, but it should start with two parts introspection, four parts, four parts learning, two more parts introspection and reconsideration, and then one part communicating your view.

The big learning I had from this project, the events of this past year, and a lifetime of mostly aimless wanderings is this trite observation: we are in this together – whether it's heaven, hell, or non-existence, we go to the same place so let's get over our belief that it is others who have biases based on fear, racism, privilege - we all have biases, biases that every human being who ever lived has. It is our lifetime calling to work through these perceptions and head in the direction of the truth.

We are critically linked/intertwined in figuring out a new path.

I think the only way to move forward is to work toward recognizing these biases and finding commonalities by finding and engaging in a dialogue one-on-one with someone we think we fundamentally disagree with – believer and atheist; Democrat and Republican, etc.

I propose we develop a tool that will do two things: 1) promote collaborative dialogue, and 2) match two people with opposing views to engage in a dialogue (i.e. the "Tinder" of constructive dialogue). If that dialogue turns out useful, the results would be shared with the community.

Who's in? Sign up at: *What.have.you.learned.so.far@gmail.com*

One love, one heart
Let's get together and feel all right
As it was in the beginning (one love)
So shall it be in the end (one heart)

(Bob Marley)

THE WHAT HAVE WE LEARNED SO FAR TEAM

This collection was written by the following amazing people: Trudy Summers, Gail Sumter, Therese Intrater, Marsha Ogden, Michelle Jackson, Mike Summers, Michael Michlowski Jr., Terri Adams, Tom King, Jennifer Jackson, Samantha Jackson, Rick Barr, Scott Sumter, Andy Lovenstein, Gary Lafree, Neil Intrater, David Chemerow, and several others who chose to remain anonymous.

The cover art is by my Mom, Erika Jackson

I learned so much from you and am inspired by your wisdom.

What fun!